No Time but Place

SUPPLY
Coca-Cola

COOP

FURNITURE
CAFE

Everyone Welcome
STRIKE NATIONAL HDQR.
FREE COFFEE..
AMERICAN AGRICULTURE
-STOP FOR IMFORMATION-
Everyone Welcome
STRIKE NATIONAL HDQR.
FREE COFFEE..
AMERICAN AGRICULTURE
-STOP FOR IMFORMATION-
AUTO
ON ITS FEET!

Jeff and Jessica Pearson

No Time but Place

A PRAIRIE PASTORAL

Photographs by JOHN W. MANOS

McGraw-Hill Book Company • New York St. Louis

San Francisco Mexico Toronto Düsseldorf

THE AUTHORS GRATEFULLY THANK Freddie for assistance and understanding beyond the call of duty; Bud and Rosalie for friendship, a place to stay, and the key to the city; Schultz and Tom for friendly criticism and helpful advice; David for an introduction to Ernest; Ernest for the chance to write and publish this book; friends in the city for putting up with our monomania for two years; and all our friends in the county for our education and their good will.

1 2 3 4 5 6 7 8 9 DODO 8 7 6 5 4 3 2 1 0

Book design by Anita Walker Scott.

Printed in the United States of America.

Published in association with SAN FRANCISCO BOOK COMPANY.

Library of Congress Cataloging in Publication Data

Pearson, Jeffrey.
No time but place.
1. Colorado—Rural conditions—Addresses, essays, lectures. 2. Country life—Colorado—Addresses, essays, lectures. I. Pearson, Jessica, joint author. II. Title.
HN79.C6P4 307.7'2'09788 80-12034
ISBN 0-07-049030-9

For Ben*—his memory—and for* Dora, Mary, *and* Bill

Contents

Preface

On Memorial Day in 1976 we quit our jobs, left our home in Denver, and moved three hundred miles away to a Dust Bowl farming community on the plains of southeastern Colorado, near the state lines of Oklahoma and Kansas. We stayed about a year, living and working and preparing this book.

We already had a few acquaintances in the community when we arrived, because Jeff had represented a group of irrigation farmers there in a lawsuit against a natural gas monopoly; but we were not prepared for surviving in such a small, isolated, physically bleak outpost of agricultural America by either education or experience. For several months, making a place for ourselves was not easy. We talked to people and participated in community life. Jeff took coffee early each morning at the cafe, went to the fields with the men, drank at the pub, attended meetings of boards, committees, lodges. Jessica went to classes in Christian Womanhood, attended salad suppers and Tupperware parties, and shopped with the women. Together we attended church, dances, banquets, and high school games. Jeff opened a solo law practice, the first in the history of the town where we settled. Jessica became a substitute teacher in the local schools.

We also tape-recorded over a hundred interviews in sessions ranging from two to fifteen hours. The interviews were typed out verbatim, and the transcripts ran from twenty to two hundred pages. A small sample of the interviews appears in this book. They are heavily edited from the original transcripts but remain true to the natural idiom of the people we spoke with.

In many ways, the community is not pleasant to live in, especially for outsiders. But by the time we left, almost a year later, we had fallen in love both with the place and with the people who live there. We had made new and, for us, unusual types of friendships. The isolation of the community forced us to develop inner resources we never knew we had. The community's strong, overt advocacy of family life—and perhaps, too, its isolation—worked on us subliminally. While there, we adopted a castaway farm dog and conceived our first child.

When we announced that we were leaving, the news traveled swiftly. Many of our new friends proved more demonstrative than we had anticipated. Both they and we, it seemed, had forgotten that our mission was limited, that in an embarrassingly fundamental sense we had never been more than voyeurs and adventurers. For a few weeks back in the city, the lights and the bustle and the traffic were disorienting. Then we began to readjust. We completed this manuscript and closed a chapter in our lives. We are retread urbanites, grateful for anonymity and amenities. We will never return, we say.

Then again, we may. A few months after we left, the farmers and ranchers in the community declared a national "farm strike." They got in touch with us, and, as their rebellion began to spread across the nation, invited us to join them. With mixed emotions we turned the invitation down. Now, although we did not return, we visit.

Our visits are like trips to a distant land only because of the roll of the odometer. They are really trips to a family, a pleasant childhood dream, an unattainable fantasy.

JEFF AND JESSICA PEARSON

Denver
January 1980

Prologue: Outside Looking Inside Out

The effort is to recognize the stature of a portion
of unimagined existence, and to contrive techniques proper
to its recording, communication, analysis, and defense.
More essentially, this is an independent inquiry into certain
normal predicaments of human divinity.

JAMES AGEE Preface to *Let Us Now Praise Famous Men*

Imagine the southern High Plains, a great physiographic province of the continental United States. Imagine the county. It is southeasternmost Colorado, but it could be the Oklahoma Panhandle. Or the Texas Panhandle. Or southwestern Kansas. Maybe even northeastern New Mexico. The county is almost perfectly square, fifty miles on a side. It is big. Vast. Five hundred square miles bigger than the state of Delaware. The climate is semiarid. The mean temperature is 53° Fahrenheit. Average rainfall is eleven inches. The county's population is 6,500; mean family income is $8,500 in a good year. There are 95,000 head of cattle and 5,000 hogs. Last year, 206 stray dogs were put to death. Four hundred traffic citations were issued. There is said to be one black family in the county, and many of the inhabitants are of Mexican descent, most of them illegal aliens who cross the border in cattle trucks for the much-coveted opportunity of mending fences and castrating cattle at $1.50 an hour. There are no traffic lights in the county. There is one church for every 272 residents.

Deep in the county there is a town. A couple of hundred families call it home. The 1970 census put the total population at a little over nine hundred, the same as it's been for the last fifteen years. The town is a child of the railroad, a complex of grain elevators, a water tower, a single paved street, inevitably named Main Street. Five blocks on either side of Main Street, town residences are platted out in a grid. Some townspeople live in modern ranch-style brick homes; others live in converted old school buses. Five feet south of the town limits is the local pub, and a mile west of the town limits is a liquor store. By local option, the town itself is as dry as if the Eighteenth Amendment had never been repealed. There is no such concept as a social drinker, but a solid conviction that hell is a real place. Farm land and pasture surround the tiny town on all sides. In section and half-section units the land shows evidence (at different times of the year) of winter wheat, corn, barley, sorghum grain, sugar beets, hay, sunflowers, oats, broomcorn, and grass.

To reach the county and the town requires traversing those flat, endless expanses of sagebrush and parched terrain and shorn crop land and newly turned earth known as the American prairie. Even in the mid-twentieth century, tens of thousands of urban Americans each year drive east across the prairie to Chicago or west to Los Angeles. On the prairie, traffic suddenly thins. Urban influences recede. As far as vision permits there is nothing but vistas of drab rolling ranch land, perfectly level crop land and cloudless blue sky. In the summer it is hot, and hot dry winds roil the dust. In the winter, it is cold and bleak. Paralleling the road is a monotonous train of power-pole crucifixes strung together with wire; here and there in the distance, the dipping pelican beak of an oil rig, the tripodal sunflower form of a windmill, the lazy convention of a cattle brood. On the radio, the familiar hype of the Top 40 yields to drawling monotones insistently reciting commodity prices and weather reports between twangy dobro harmonies and songs about old-fashioned, unrequited love. The radio complements perfectly the brutal homogeneity of the panorama. The empty horizon lures the traveler on.

For those not too numbed to notice, the passing parade of traffic begins to tell a story of another society, another world. The city's fuel-injected compacts and sporty imports give way to mud-splattered pickups with rifle racks and bumper stickers saying "Eat Beef" or "Skoal, Brother"; heavy bobtail trucks with bright red siding, hauling mountains of sandlike grain; long semi-pulled trailer trucks packed with corpulent cattle. Now and then an American-made standard, gas-guzzling sedan with a surfeit of shiny chrome and a CB antenna on the back rumbles by.

Every ten or twenty miles an asymmetrical bulge begins to grow on the horizon. As the bulge gets larger and larger, a sign commands to reduce speed. For a few unpleasant kaleidoscopic instants the traveler glimpses desolate symbols of what is surely a peopled but uncivilized settlement. There is no town square, no verdant common, no tidy row of gabled clapboard homes. Instead, a few cement block buildings with pickups herring-boned in front of them. A sign boasting "Home Cooked Eats." A filling station, pot-bellied geezers in cowboy hats lounging by the pumps. A side street lined with what look like unpainted barns, metal sheds, a few scraggly trees, playing children. A mobile home and a rusted tractor cab by the side of the road. A cement silo elevator and a water tower looming up over everything else. A moment later, signs advise speed can be resumed. The town is over. The prairie continues.

This is the Great American Dust Bowl, a land rendered vaguely romantic and allegorical by the ballads of Woody Guthrie and the novels of John Steinbeck. Here lie the county and the town. Once this prairie was inhabited exclusively by grazing ruminants, their roughneck cowboy overseers, and outlaw rustlers. Then, in a rush stimulated by the promise of free land and plenty, there came farmers. They came as far as they could by rail; and then they walked and traveled in Conestoga wagons, determined, land-hungry adventurers seduced into the land's anonymous vastness the way sailors are lured to sea. Once in the county, these adventurers, finding no trees, burrowed into the ground like gophers. The holes that became their shelters they called dugouts, and into these muddy dungeons they packed their families and hope chests and quilts, and in them they dreamed of freedom and prosperity. All but a few of the dugouts have now been plowed over and planted to wheat, corn, or milo.

The farmers quickly clashed with the cowboys and cattlemen. They ripped the sod with horse-drawn plows and erected fences where there had only been open range. They insisted on rights-of-way and frowned on trespassing; many a stray cattle-company steer found its way to the farmer's dinner table. For a few years the land beneath the ripped sod yielded bountiful harvests. Word traveled fast. More adventurers poured in. They came from the South and from the North, but mainly from the South, bringing with them a hodgepodge of peculiar names. The women were called such as Armilda, Reba, Wynema, Alma, Quineth, Ina, Ludie, Mertye, Beulah, Minta, Alta, Trine, Bronyn, Joma, Corlena, Zela, Nim, Marvadene, Lumira, Opal, Nila, Colma, Cyncia, and Vernelle. The men were called by names like Oran, Oezell, Pinley, Othe, Murl, Hays, Norland, Arlon, Arwin, Irl, Ogle, Karis, Alva, Rhoten, Zolin, Gwiney, Obed, Arden, Coy, Verle, and Dorsey. They were a hardy people but even so were unprepared for the simple but devastating secret of this vast land, unveiled with the passing of years: rain is always followed by no rain, fat years by lean. The sun and the wind and the dryness drove the farmers out. The rains came. The farmers returned. Drought displaced them. In and out, back and forth. Today, scientists say there is a twenty-year drought cycle. The Dry Teens were followed by the Dirty Thirties, the Dirty Thirties by the Filthy Fifties. In the Eighties, the dirt is again swirling across the prairie, and the crops and cattle are languishing in dust.

People adapt or leave. Most leave. Their children leave. There is a better life almost anywhere else. A few stay. "Born here and never had the money to leave," they say. Such heavy-handed irony, such a proud people. No amount of money in the world would make *them* leave. Staying has become a mission, a test, a value in itself. Those who have endured are as parched of surface tenderness as the land itself, as fanatically defiant of the biting winds as Lear. They are sinewy like the coyote, calculating like the prairie rattler. Their humanity is as inscrutable as the subsurface soil, the rich sandy loam in which anything, but anything will grow with a little moisture. They are plodding, unsentimental, ahistorical souls who have built a civilization out of mud and straw and baling wire. They know how sweet life is when it is spent close to death. Each joust with nature, each tragedy and catastrophe teaches more about death. Surviving is a sweetly morbid experience.

Back in the 1940s, the county was the broomcorn capital of the world. Were it not for synthetics and the high price of labor, it still could be today, for the fruitless corn plants from which brooms are made grow well in sandy soils rich in nutrients. In the boom days of broomcorn, the county was overrun with Indians and skid-row winos (later, *braceros* and skid-row winos), wandering, homeless men who cut and seeded and baled the hardy broomcorn plants by hand. They knifed each other on Saturday night, drank and gambled their money away, stood in long lines for the picture show, and often departed in cattle trucks as penniless as they had come. In the 1950s, when synthetics cornered the broom market and the broomcorn broom magnates moved to Mexico, the boom ended. Farmers took to growing whatever the people in the city told them to grow. The humming steel rails of the railroad passed on messages: Try sugar beets. Try onions. Try pinto beans. Some county boosters mistakenly thought these labor-intensive crops would revive the local economy, bring back the boom. Actually, labor costs got higher and higher, and the local economy slumped.

Then the same burst of postwar American genius that made broomcorn obsolete solved the labor problem and almost eliminated the droughts. Engineers designed tractors and combines that did more and more of the farmer's work; botanists and chemists developed seeds and fertilizers to double, triple, quadruple the production of corn. Farmers in Iowa may have been the intended beneficiaries of these scientific and technological breakthroughs, but farmers in the county cashed in on them too. At the same time, geologists discovered huge aquifers hundreds of feet beneath the prairie's surface; pumps and engines were devised to suck the water out, huge derrick rigs to penetrate the depths.

For a time it looked as if the county was entering a new era of prosperity. Tremendous tracts of blow land and sand hills suddenly bloomed with feed crops. The growing season doubled: corn and the grain sorghum people in the county call milo (or, sometimes, maize) could be planted in the spring and harvested in the fall before frost; winter wheat could be planted just before corn harvest in the fall and harvested in the middle of the summer, just when the corn was tasseling. Having a stable supply of local grain, cattlemen stopped shipping their yearlings two thousand miles to Midwest feedyards and auctions. Instead, they built scientific feeding centers right in the county, where thousands of lean range critters each year could gorge to obesity on mixtures of corn, milo, cottonseed hulls, hay, molasses, vitamins, and DES hormones concocted by the biologists and chemists. Americans proved just as willing to gorge; beef sales rose, and county farmers and ranchers rushed to meet the demand. The rangemen bred larger and larger herds; matched exotic sires to exotic dams to calve bigger and bigger calves; put more and more yearlings into the feedlots. The feedlot managers pushed the cattle harder and harder, and soon the animals were gaining two or more pounds a day and consuming twenty or more pounds of feed a day to do it. To offset increasing investments in machinery and chemicals and irrigation equipment, farmers acquired larger holdings and plowed under even greater expanses of buffalo grass. Production became a creed, bigness and efficiency its practical manifestations.

But nature, agribusiness, and that complex web of contingencies known as the free market did not cooperate for the long-term benefit of the county. Pressure dropped in good wells; sandy sediment appeared in the water. Today, wells have to be drilled to a thousand feet where once they were drilled to the hundreds. Fuel bills soar; thousands of dollars a month go to drive the irrigation engines. The day is fast approaching when the raucous diesels on the prairie will fall silent, when the creeping center-pivot sprinklers will grind to a stop and the gated irrigation pipe will lie rusting on the ground. All over the country, bigness and efficiency have created commodity surpluses; year after year of bumper corn and wheat crops have filled farm storage bins and driven corn and wheat prices far below the cost of production while the cost of steel equipment and oil and chemical inputs continues to rise. County farmers and ranchers are confused. Is this the reward for hard work? For long hours and frugality and efficiency?

The questions are unanswerable, but they provoke outpourings of self-pity and cynicism among the county farmers. The government no longer cares about farmers, they say. Washington responds only to freeloading urban labor and other organized interests. Labor won't let us sell our wheat to the Russians. Labor yelps about imported shoes but responds with silence to the processing of foreign beef in Puerto Rico to circumvent import quotas. Consumers in the cities boycott American beef just when the returns are beginning to pay off the investment. Why do consumers pick on the producer? Why don't "they" boycott new automobiles or Hamburger Helper? "They" don't realize that they eat the best food in the world at the lowest prices in the world and it won't be long until they drive the small producer completely out of business. Some day, the AFL-CIO will be dictating the price of a T-bone. And they will get exactly what they deserve.

But the reckless adventurers turned stubborn survivalists continue to farm and ranch, spawning new generations who vow to leave in their youth and end up—some of them—staying forever. The old-timers are now cash poor and capital rich; the modest farms and ranches they began buying up before, during, and after the Great Depression are now worth half a million, a million, two million dollars. More than ever before, sons depend on fathers to enter the business, fathers on sons to stay in it; and father and son alike are precariously perched on an eroding ledge of outmoded values above a great chaotic abyss of economic reality. It is perhaps no surprise that farmers and ranchers in the county get along with each other better than they did in the early sod-busting days. They deal with the same incomprehensibly volatile international market forces; they are tormented by the same suspicions of conspiracy on the Mercantile Exchange and the Board of Trade, by the same visceral rage every time a labor leader opens his mouth or the workers at International Harvester go out on strike. They wear the same cowboy hats and drive the same pickups from dawn to nightfall. Most importantly, they dream the same dreams. For the old-time cow puncher, for the young laborer at the feedyard pulling a squeeze chute all day long, for the hired hand in the tractor cab, for the small rancher at the sale barn watching his cattle go for less than he paid for them, for the small farmer nervously approaching his banker for another extension of his note—for all of them, the dream is still just cows and calves and your own place and being free. Blindly, reflexively, they cling to the dream, cling so obsessively that dream and reality become confused. The illusion of independence is everywhere. No matter that independence means paying whatever price the corporate conglomerates decide is right in the monopolistic marketplace of agricultural inputs. No matter that independence means taking whatever price you can get for your product from the handful of integrated beef and grain processors that controls the wholesale market. In agriculture, the illusion declares, a man is still his own boss.

The power of illusion is part of what makes the county a holding reservoir for classical American agrarianism. As if tutored in physiocratic doctrine by Quesnay himself, every man, woman, and child in the county grows up believing the products of the earth to be the only true forms of wealth. On agriculture rests the success of every other industry. Almost smugly, parents assert that the farm is the only decent place to raise children. Hard work is the exclusive achievement of agriculturalists; private property is nowhere so sacred as it is on the farm; city life is demonic and devious. The county never has been and never will be egalitarian or democratic, but every county native is as certain as Thomas Jefferson that agricultural yeomanry is the last, single guarantee of freedom.

Remoteness and environmental harshness protect the county's insularity. Intrusions are few and carefully controlled by distance and nature's inclemency. Farm technology trickles in. Other manifestations of the material culture of the outside world are coveted, imitated, sometimes actually acquired. But for the most part, and especially on the byways of consciousness, the outside world passes by unheeded. It could be 1910. It could be 1939. It could be 1952. It could be notime. The county is unaccounted for, economically dispensable, cut off from the twentieth century. The wind blows, but it is not a wind of change. The dust blows with it, but beneath the topsoil the land remains the same. Children are born, loans fall due, men go insane. It has been ever thus.

In this peculiarly vestigial world, collectivities are vehicles for identity, pride, ontological significance. Away from their families, church groups, sports teams, and communities, individuals do not exist. Surname inexorably condemns or redeems. Blood relations are friends and business partners. The male trades his fiduciary responsibilities to the family for the domestic labor of his spouse; the male is the provider, the female the housekeeper. His is a world of tool-littered pickups, burning crops, cafe gossip, tobacco, and evenings in front of the television console. Hers is a world of children, hot meals, seeping dust, catalog shopping, and glasses of iced tea with the Avon lady on a quiet afternoon. Rarely do the two worlds intersect.

What the family is for the individual, the local school is for the community. Its emblems, teams, and accomplishments inspire more loyalty in the populace than does the nation-state. This is passing strange, for by any objective standard the school is a dismal failure. It does not offer foreign language courses; it is a notorious way station for inexperienced teachers unable to find jobs elsewhere; it has failed to produce even a small cohort of accomplished college students. But unlike any other community institution, the school persists in involving both the young and the old in the celebration of belonging. In a community forsaken by the rest of the world, it is important to belong.

The importance of belonging is manifested somewhat differently in the county's religious life. The county is a place where leather-bound Bibles are standard coffee-table decor, where reproductions of the Last Supper hang side by side with mail-order western prints in the family room, where Sunday morning means little girls dressed in pink organdy and lace and little boys in string ties and neat western outfits. Man's spiritual life consists of fearing the devil, dreading hell, and deciding whether to accept the Lord Jesus Christ with childlike faith. When little boys and little girls reach five or six, they are eligible to accept. To become Christians. In the county, a Christian is no mere Gentile. A Christian is born again, saved, assured of eternal life. A Christian is one for whom life's hardships and joys, its births and deaths, and its droughts and rains are to be met with equanimity. All is part of His design. There is no such thing as a tormented soul. Accepting the Lord is as uncomplicated as marching forward during the invitation at Sunday service or at a revival in the gymnasium. Rejecting Him is as uncomplicated as drinking coffee or spending an evening at the roadhouse in the county seat. A county Christian is forbiddingly self-assured, but he is rarely influential in matters worldly.

Those with secular influence are the landed, the tenured, the persevering, their influence measured by how long ago their family came and how tenaciously they scrimped, acquired, and boosted the county in its hours of need. It is impossible to be influential in the county without being an old-timer; it is impossible to be an old-timer without having a grandfather who died there. The powerful do not flaunt their power. Rich and poor alike subscribe to the Lockean notion that he who is least governed is best governed. Justice is private and informal. County leaders hold court in the cafe or the grain elevator or at the feedlot; they never run for elective office, although they may determine what the elected officials decide to do. Federal and state bureaucracies are remote irrelevancies. The unfortunate bureaucrat who ventures to assert the outside world's jurisdiction over county affairs is quickly expelled, sometimes by force. In the county they do things the way they always have and the way they damn well please.

Years and generations seem to melt into each other. Genealogies become more complicated but rarely less capable of being traced within a hundred-mile radius of the county's center. As people there say, folks just get by. Life is mostly work and routine. Of course, there is always the ball game or the wrestling match on Friday and Saturday night. There is the picture show, the Legion club just outside the town's limits, the roadhouses in other towns, the foosball machines at the teen center, and the glorious sweep of the town's principal thoroughfare that the kids call "dragging Main." There are beer parties at the cemetery and lodge meetings in abandoned schoolhouses; there is Wednesday night prayer meeting. Every so often there are big cowboy dances at the gymnasium.

Nevertheless, a certain vague restiveness stalks the county. It is not wholesale nostalgia, not by any means. No one wants to go back to driving tractors without air conditioning, hydrostatics, tape decks, and cushioned seats. No one wants to go back to living in a dugout. No one wants to go back to checking cattle on horseback, to branding in the open in the mud rather than in the squeeze chute. Yet the old farmers and ranchers sometimes fret that the pace of life is becoming too hurried. People are busier than they used to be, more preoccupied with prices and returns than with visiting and "neighboring." Television has all but pre-empted the old forms of affirming collectivity. The closest thing to a church pie social or a ciphering match today is the high school varsity game. The youngsters spend more time in school sports activities and in their cars on the Main Street drag than they do farming or working cattle. There are drugs about; divorce, illegitimacy, and cuckoldry assault the ranks of the better sort of folks. Big-shot doctors and lawyers who don't know which end of a cow the hay goes in infiltrate the county in the guise of syndicated partnerships, driving up land prices and suckering local retail merchants. Inheritance taxes jeopardize one's God-given right to pass the ground on to the children. Farm girls turned farm wives, liberated by a measure of prosperity, jubilantly trade domestic slavery to be shoppers and consumers and find the trade unsatisfying.

In the fall of 1977 the building tidal wave of the outside agricultural economy broke brutally upon the county's insularity. Commodity prices dipped to their lowest parity position since the Depression, and the new administration in Washington offered a farm bill that promised no relief. In the county, restiveness turned to rebellion. The county's practitioners of commercial botany and animal husbandry suddenly perceived that market forces and government programs—enemies far more treacherous than droughts and winds—threatened their dreams and illusions. They refused to accept their dispensability. In one angry and spontaneous mass they threw themselves bodily at the present. In the little Dust Bowl county on the prairie the American Agriculture Movement was born.

The American Agriculture Movement has sent tractors through the streets and farmers through the halls of Congress. It has captured the imagination of rural America and precipitated the largest outbreak of nationwide agrarian protest since the Farmers' Holiday Movement of 1932.

But that is—or in time will be—history. The task here is to chronicle a portion of unimagined existence. And a place. Imagine now this land where few outsiders venture. Imagine the winds, the droughts, the fine granules of dust in the food. Imagine the people, the grease and starch in their diets, the hellfire in their religions, the determination in their eyes, the urgency of their cheers for the team.

Abe Berkowitz: A Yokel Myself

This Jew boy (he points to himself). If they didn't have this Jew boy, they'd have no picture show. And when I'm gone, they probably won't have no show in this town.

Shrugs, flips of the arms, snorts, large ears and nose, thick lips, thick Yiddish accent, fedora, shirts buttoned to the neck with no necktie, double-knit suits from faraway K-Marts. Abe Berkowitz, who grew up in New York City, is the county's oddest oddball, an outsider's insider. One Sunday several months before we move to the county to stay, we drop by his little bungalow on Main Street and introduce ourselves. Wall-to-wall shag, plastic-covered recliners, a large commercial painting of Jesus on the wall (Abe's present wife is an Okie, born-again). Abe is in a dressing gown. When he learns Jessica is Jewish, he warms quickly. He marvels that Jeff plans to open a law practice in the old irrigation equipment parts supply garage on Main Street. The garage is next door to Abe's Ace Theater, a big, metal Quonset-hut building. "A lawyer!" he shouts. "You crazy?" He shakes his head in disbelief. "In this little two-bit town? I never thought I'd live to see the day."

He takes us on a tour of the theater building before the Sunday matinee. He shows off the glassed-in, soundproofed Cry Room near the ladies' lounge "for mommas and babies." He has just remodeled the auditorium—new industrial carpeting down the aisles, new upholstery on the seats, a fresh coat of deck paint on the cement floor under the seats—but the projection room has not been touched. Carbide rods are still used to fuel the projection lamp.

Seven days a week Abe and his Okie wife shlep the vacuum sweeper up and down the aisles of the Ace Theater, pop the popcorn, repair the ice machine, and greet the clientele at the door. Abe is now seventy-seven, the only Jew in the county.

COMING
NEXT ATTRACTION
WED. - THURS. - FRI. - SAT.
4 BIG DAYS
He freed his mind and body to commit the most sensual and shocking acts imaginable!
ADMISSION
ADULT

We want to learn his story. After we have moved to the town to stay, we try repeatedly to interview him. He is happy to chat, but he resists the interview. We bring him homemade chopped liver. We frequent his picture show. We telephone. We drop in unannounced. Nothing works. One day, for no apparent reason, he volunteers to face the tape recorder. We meet him in the lobby of the Ace Theater. He sits behind the ticket counter. We learn very quickly it's not the tape recorder he's resisting. He is resisting memories.

I often sat in a theater. (He pauses.) I can remember. And I said, "Someday I'm gonna have a theater." I did.

I broke into the business back in New York, see. Seventh Avenue. And I wasn't on the payroll. I was just a flunky, see, for this distribution company. My office was downstairs, the lobby. When they wanted a job done, they'd get me, call me. Pay me good. And I did it. So one day this guy says, "Come upstairs, I want to talk to you." They had a pretty good picture that they partially owned. And they distributed it throughout the United States. I can remember the picture as plain as day. It was a jungle picture. Jungle pictures seemed to go over pretty good then. So the owner of this laboratory calls me in, tells me I can have this territory out west for this jungle picture. So it's a long story. I said, "I'll let you know." He said, "Move out there, you'll make a lot of money." I'd just got married to my first wife. She's got a good job, she's the breadwinner. So, to make a long story short, I talked to her, and she said okay. So I moved out west. And I stayed. Went into the Navy, got out, and I was starving. Out of luck. So along comes this tip. This part of the country is open. Some guy is looking to sell a theater.

So I went to see this guy. Hey, you think this town is crummy now. You should have seen it when I came here.

It was enough to give you the itch. I wasn't too happy. (He shakes his head.) Well, I'm trying to be truthful. "God," I says to this guy, "you know it takes a lot of people to support a theater." Well, this guy's quick reply to me was, "Don't you worry," he says. "You give the people what they want, and they'll patronize you." Well, I figure this guy's gone to all that expense to erect this metal building, he must know what he's doing. So I picked it up. I figured this guy can't be so stupid if he's invested all this money. He can't be so stupid. The guy that's really stupid is the guy that doesn't have anything. That's the guy that's stupid. And that was me, see? I didn't have anything. So I said, "How much would you want for rent?" He said, "I don't know." He said, "How much will you pay?" So I said, "I don't know, either." Anyway, I chased the guy for eleven months to find out what the rent was. So finally I caught him. And I'm still paying the same rent today. 'Course, he's passed on, and I'm paying it to the estate.

It wasn't very cheerful looking back then. We hardly had any street lights. If you think this place looks bad now, this is marvelous. (He snorts and laughs at the same time.) You just come from New York, any big city. You come down here to live. This is the other side of the world. Most people, they'd have to put you in a padded cell. I tell you, it takes a lot of nerve to stay here. But I guess it grows on you. You get so damned used to it. I don't know any different now. I guess I'm a yokel myself. . . .

To this day, I can remember very clearly that everybody thought I'd just come out here, open it up, and sell it out. And leave. Since that day, it's been thirty years come July. (He breaks down in convulsive sobs; the tape recorder is turned off, and Jessica gives him tissues.) It's . . . rather touching . . . but . . . here I am. (He pauses, reflective.) After a lot of hard work . . . disappointments . . . it finally opened up at the end of July 1946. It was just a business for me at the start. You figure, well, you'll get the hell out someday. I'd think things like that, sure. But it never was too hard to take. I'm sincere about that. Never too hard to take. What the hell good's beautiful scenery somewhere else if you haven't got a pot to pee in? What good is it?

But this is a business you can be in all your life, and you just can't predict. There's only one fellow I knew that could predict, and he was an Irishman. We were partners when I was in the service.

Are Irishmen as smart as Jews?

You bet. They're a lot smarter. A lot smarter. The Jews can't get near 'em. And the goys can get away with more than the Jews can. Know what I mean?

What's it like being a Jew here? I know people have laughed occasionally when I've told them my maiden name.

You're opposite, see? See, I got an Okie. You got him. (He points at Jeff and laughs.) No, you gotta be careful. When I first came here, I don't think people knew what a Jew was. Maybe they thought I had horns. But they never did bother me. I done the right thing, that's all. I wouldn't ever hide it. No, I'm too proud. The hell with ya. You don't like me, just go shit in the attic. I don't give a damn. No, I told you. I'm the only one in the county that admits it.

You miss Yiddishkeit?

You miss it, yeah. I don't want to act like I ever took advantage of my religion. I never lived it. But you know what you are. That don't mean you've got to live it. I'm married to a Gentile lady, so we just eliminate that. She never says anything, and I don't say anything. That's how we get along. So what the heck, we're all human. That's what counts. That's all. Sometimes, somebody says something. So what are you going to do? Anybody who talks like that is ignorant, right? You going to try to smarten' 'em up? To hell with 'em. Let 'em be stupid.

But these people are fine people. When my first wife died, I realized how many friends I had here. All sorts of people. Friends I never knew I had. They sent cards, contributions. Jews don't have flowers, you know. I sent all the money to a rabbi. No, they're good people. They've supported this theater no end. In all the years I've been here, I've always tried to furnish 'em the best entertainment Hollywood provides. They like Westerns. And comedies. And we play all the Walt Disneys. I always give 'em the best. This is the God's honest truth. Always will as long as I'm here. They're good people. A little stupid, maybe, but they're all right. By stupid, I mean not educated. What the hell, though, they're smart in their way. Maybe a person is better off living in a place like this. Nothing to worry about, nothing to bother you, don't need a key for your house door . . . nobody going to slug you on the street. (He snorts.) I've been away from the likes of civilization so long, I don't know what it's like anymore. They say New York is taken over by the Puerto Ricans.

But you know what's wrong with this town? I'll tell you what's wrong with this town. Both those goddamn food markets. You buy there?

We try to support the local merchants.

You're a horse's banana. You know what I buy here? I buy bread. Or in the summertime, if it's warm, I buy milk, stuff like that. Go over to the county seat Friday or

Saturday, either one of the food markets there, you'll see mainly people from here. Go somewhere in Kansas, you'll see the same thing. These two markets with their prices, they're hurting this town. I don't buy nothing here. They know that I eat, my wife eats. They know that we buy something. I go in there, I come out with a loaf of bread, I say, "Please deliver this to my residence." (He laughs.) Just kidding them. They must know I'm buying meat somewhere. If they ask me, I'll tell them. We go to Amarillo. My God, I bet you we pay for the trip in the difference there is with the stuff we bring back, just on small items. And the meat here, you can't eat it. Do you try to eat it? No good, right? No good. I don't know what they're doing. They're just driving people out. You'd think they'd see that's not good for the town.

I tell you, if I was a young man and not in show business, I'd take that cafe up the street and make some money. Not a decent place to eat in the whole goddamn place. But you can't get no help. And there's no good cooks. They're all like my old lady, my wife now: grease monkeys. My wife now was a cook when I met her here. A fine Okie cook, fine for this town. That's saturation cooking what they do here. I don't let her cook for me. I cook my own breakfast. So I eat my fancy New York style. That's what she calls it. I says, "Okay, I'll eat New York, you eat this grease." So she gets sick eating grease. (He chuckles.) Anybody eat that kind of damn grease, you'll get sick. The eggs swim to the bacon, the bacon swims to the eggs. Yecccchhh.

But this is a changing town. We used to have big harvests here, broomcorn harvests. That was the big thing here. You couldn't walk down Main Street, it was so full of Indians. Harvesting broomcorn. You had to stand in line to the corner to get in this theater. (He makes a broad sweep with one arm.) I said this town was very kind to me, right? Well, that was it. But broomcorn was less and less, and now it's nothing. That's why we need something here. But nobody cares here. You know what they care about here? Football. More football. Basketball, baseball. That's all. They're ball crazy. No learning. Ignorant. I betcha at graduation there isn't half a dozen that's college material. I don't think there's one of 'em. They don't know how to make out a check when they're juniors, seniors. I tell 'em, "Just sign it." Teach the little bastards. I'm not kidding. In New York, you went to school to learn something, right? I know I did. Here, this is a joke. This is drek. They're too busy with the ball-playing. Five nights, six nights a week.

What's it like running the picture show in such a small town?

I'll tell it to you straight. You can't do in a small town like you do in a big city. You can't be a big boss. You gotta do most of the work yourself. If we had to have a manager for this theater, there'd be no theater here. You gotta do everything. My wife does the cleaning, I do this and that. The only one you hire is the projectionist. Some kid, that's all. It's a part-time job. They're tickled to death. Our admission is still $1.50. Cheap. And most of the people appreciate it. You can't charge these people too much, you know what I mean? These people, you see them every day. In the big city, if you don't have one *toochis* sitting in the seat, it's another one. Don't make any difference what you charge. Here, it's a small town. It's the same *toochis* in the seat. You can't charge 'em too much. Last night, we took in $18.00 and change. That's all. Costs me forty some odd dollars just to open the doors. But you make that up, see. I'm not crying. Don't get me wrong.

But my first wife couldn't take this life. Just couldn't

take it. It didn't do her any good down here. She was sick when I brought her here, and she died of cancer. It was rough, a rough, rough battle. This business gets monotonous, seven days a week, no holidays. Now I'm trying to sell. But this is a hard country to sell anything. No go-getters. And this is a hard business to sell. Somebody's in the business, they look at this town and they get sick. (He chuckles.) Where do you think a guy comes from who wants to open up in this town? You'd think he's crazy buying the show. That's right.

My first wife's been dead about sixteen years. That's the last time I was back in New York. I don't know New York now. But before I cash in my chips, I'm going back. I was born on East Eighty-eighth Street, see? In a brownstone. I want to go back and just see Eighty-eighth Street. Walk up and down.

If you had the chance, how would you live life differently?

I can't answer that. That's hard. You can't answer that question. And ask me where the money went. I don't know. Where the hell did the money go? I don't know. I'm not broke, I'll tell you that much. But they got me down as a millionaire. (He gestures carelessly at the world outside the theater's glass front doors.) No. (He laughs and shakes his head.) I tell you, if you only knew then what you knew now, you'd be all right. You gotta learn it the hard way. When I left New York to come out west, I was going to show these yokels. Well, if the truth is known, they showed me.

What will I do when I sell out? I don't know what I'll do when I sell out. Who cares what I do after that? Who cares? When you wake up at seventy-seven, you say "Dear God, thank you." So how many thanks you gotta give?

1 ❧ *Settings*

We saw outside our window
Where wheatfields they had grown,
Was now a rippling ocean
Of dust the wind had blown

WOODY GUTHRIE "Dust Storm Disaster"*

That old dust might killed my wheat, boys,
But it can't kill me, Lord,
It can't kill me.

WOODY GUTHRIE "Dust Can't Kill Me"*

THE LAND

Draw a line down the middle of the county, north to south. To the west, cattle country: grasslands, mesas, canyons, cedar-spiked hills. To the east, farm country: uplands so flat the naked eye cannot perceive the terrain's negative slope, west to east, a foot or two feet every mile. Along the west to east declension are creeks, streams, rivers, ravines, arroyos. They are all dry, watercourses cured of surface water by the ages. White settlers came to the eastern half of the county, struggled with the soil, and stayed; brought cattle and sheep to the western half of the county and struggled to stay.

The cowman drove out the shepherd years ago and with him the cross-twined, meshed wire fences. Now, along the unoiled, winding county roads and the cattle-guarded, dusty, private ranch trails that squirm through the western half of the county there is four-strand barbed wire, slung up on knotted, bleached, twisted posts of old cedar or pinion or (best of all, some say) pear apple tree. The fences wing the roads, then streak off up mesas or down into ravines, crawl out of sight over the horizon and behind scruffy hills. The ground cover in the draws and over the tamer uplands, where the cattle graze, the basic ground cover, is buffalo grass; it grows close to the ground in mangy clumps as small as half dollars and as big as potholders. It is generally the color of the earth itself and very dry. But after a good rain, it may turn a soft yellow. After a very good rain, it may just slightly hint at the palest of olive greens.

A very good rain sprouts filaments of grama grass and western wheat grass and colonies of sunflowers. Still, the stoutest, most dependable feed of all is the buffalo grass. With a little moisture in the fall it comes back strong in the spring, year after year, and the worst of droughts will not kill it. Of course, whether it rains or not, there are always scrub cedar and sagebrush; little elephant-ear cacti, cropped close to the ground; spiked soapweed cacti; and cholla cacti, spindly little bushes bearing prickly bulbs of sticky, rich meat on their lean, twining tentacles; poverty weed and pigweed. It is a land of harsh contrasts. Scarps of crumbling rock ascend picturesque mesas capped with ill-fitting toupees of dark cedar or pinion. Down in the rugged canyons that secure many of the ranch houses, across rock crossing where water sometimes flows and past the tiny patches of maize that ranchers half-heartedly cultivate there may be quiet glens of cottonwood and chinaberry. In the air, soaring white-tailed eagles and families of quail. On the ground, roadrunners, coyotes, fox squirrels, wild turkeys, badgers, ferrets, coons, antelope, rattlesnakes, bull snakes, and an occasional bobcat.

The cattle summer on the uplands and winter in the canyons. Where the ranchers are, or have been, windmills: phlegmatic, gawking sentries, defenseless giants, blinking eyeless eyelids at the wind and soughing and creaking through decades, battered, paintless, and lonely, legs straddled over rusted corrugated watering tanks. And the ruminants: specks in the distance, sprinkled pebbles on the horizon, or fat, fleecy mobs sulking around the windmill's graceless straddled legs, converting food, ten to forty acres each, stumbling, loafing, defecating, waiting for something to happen without expectation, apprehension, or memory; bred in the summer, born in the spring, culled and weaned in the fall, shipped, grazed, or re-bred according to concepts never explained, such as rate of gain, futures, bloodline, weaning weight, Australian imports, conformation. Mixed crews of black, red, brown, white, yellow, loiterers all.

At sunset, ranch trails and county roads are deserted. Every five to ten miles, tails of ranch-house smoke twirl upward into the powder blue sky and are lost, the ranch houses invisible, secreted in safe canyons. Canyons where grandfathers built homesteads, negotiated grazing permits, planted cottonwoods and chinaberries so men could stay. And be proud. And erect proud gateways to their castles, using arc welders, horseshoes, and pipe. The gateways introduce the home place, proclaiming surnames and brands and the first names of living, breathing husbands, wives, and children. Smoke curling, powder blue heavens, powder blue haze. Pastel streaks of pink and orange flicker in the crimson blaze on the western horizon, but the blaze is short-lived. A tidal wave of murky, bruised purple-blueness surges and swells westward, banking the pinks and oranges and crimson. Suddenly, darkness: cloudless, star-pricked skies.

East of the imaginary north-south line splitting the county in half the farmer rules. The rolling terrain stops. The hills are gone. The mesas have disappeared. In every direction, as far as the eye can see, even molding, sky joined neatly to earth. Emptiness. A country created to define vastness. The open range about which songs are written, transformed by homesteading policies, technology, and markets into expansive tables supporting tillage and row cropping. There are more miles of oiled blacktop. There are more county roads. There are more private roads. The roads define sections and townships and ranges: a perfect, symmetrical grid; a patchwork quilt from the air; a logical, predictable navigation system on the ground.

The farmers broke the sod in the east half and chased the cowman to the western part of the county, where the cowman drove out the shepherd. The big drought and the Depression punished the sodbreakers and chased them willy-nilly in four directions. When the men in the cities discovered water deeper than the water in artesian wells, built bigger tractors and stronger tools, and turned natural fuels into fertilizer, the farmers returned.

The litter of decades of the farmers' civilization is seen in the open spaces: power lines, highline poles, telephone

lines, crumbling foundations of abandoned stone schoolhouses, arched gateways of old cemeteries for towns that have died, feedlot feed mills, windmills, isolated farmsteads, and, way out where sky meets land, small rows of plugs sticking up like electronic tubes on a flat panel. Elevators. The elevators are big and cylindrical and tall; they are made of cement, stuck together, and plopped by the tracks. At the top they announce the names of towns and the names of corporations: Bunge, Bartlett, Gano, Co-Op. The railroad cars glide by them and pick up and deliver, West to East, East to West; Atchison, Topeka & Santa Fe grain-hopper cars recline on sidings, attending buy-sell decisions, brokerage terms, secondary market financing, terminal market prices.

And the towns. They are anchored into civilization by the inverted pilings of sixty-foot television antennas, communal cousins of the windmills, receptors of news, pap, and excitement from cities in two, three, or four states. The towns are hunkering assemblages of single-story refuges from wind and dust, of trailer homes, of metal-frame businesses, of cement-block Main Streets, of shingled-over sod hovels, shacks, frame houses, prosperous ranch-style brick comfort palaces, winterized school buses, railroad cars. Everywhere is the debris of post-World War II machine-age scrimping—backyard junk piles, vacant-lot junk piles, junk-pile junk piles. Lumber is still as scarce as ever, but corrugated metal has supplanted the sod and tarpaper: for farmers' barns, shops, storage bins, loafing sheds, farrowing houses; for merchants' stores and showrooms, veterinarians' offices, grain dealers' overflow, and showmen's theaters. The homely metal material comes in blue, brown, and pink besides its natural steel gray, and in three geometrical solids: box, cone, and roundtop (Quonset-hut progeny, arched semicircles in cross-section).

Mile-long section lines separate county farmsteads, discernible by high-intensity barn lights at night, hand-planted rows of shelter trees by day. Around the farmsteads, more machine-age debris. Rusted vehicle hulls, drills, plows, sweeps, disks, tractors, combines, grain carts, fence wire spools. The past is joined to the present by baling wire and ancestors' surviving handi-work: decrepit jerrybuilt corrals, abandoned brooding sheds, pump houses, blacksmith huts, wells. Nothing ventured but its predecessor saved, plucked over, and left to decay. And around the farmsteads the flat land, deceptive in its sameness, undergoes cyclical transformations.

The land is most glorious in June. In a good year, there are fields of ripe, harvest-ready, picturebook golden wheat; stands of baby green corn or milo, foot-high, poking up tentative stalks and leaves from the bottoms of deep, wide irrigation furrows, furrows flooded with hundreds, sometimes thousands, of gallons of water per minute. The land is sorriest in the winter, good years and bad, when the earth is bleached brown and bleak; when the cattle stoically graze the amputated stalks of fall-harvested corn and milo; when the once-fuzzy green carpet of fall-drilled wheat struggles dully through the freeze; when the unworked ground of farmers on furlough lifts up with the wind, disperses, and re-forms in wind-driven clouds that terrorize nature, man, and beast.

In between the sorrow and the glory, rich, brown wheat ground in the fall prior to drilling: uniformly turned, patterned, sealing up moisture and nutrients beneath its man-made scratches. Tall, ripe, forest-thick rows of green August corn. Intractable wastelands of bindweed, Johnson grass, shattercane, and the ravages of greenbug and rootworm. Uneven stands of mature milo, drying naturally for harvest, comical amber and russet heads of grain swaying and periscoping erratically atop three- and four-foot bodies. Scorched, black wheat ground, successor to burned-off harvest stubble. Failed crops and partially failed crops ready to be turned over and planted to the crop of next year's hopes. Flooded fields of furrowed row crops, standing pools of unused precious tail water, weedy barrow ditches, fence rows, and railroad rights-of-way. Green wheat fuzz in November, sprinkled with powdered sugar of dry blowing snow.

It is the land of the unexpected, ruled by men surprised neither by extremes nor by norms. Each generation, each year, men expect and accept.

Poe Jones: The Curiosity of Nature

Let me tell you something that's really funny. My full name is Edgar Allan Poe Jones, and I was born on April the 15th: income tax day.

It is Poe Jones' studio, and he and I are alone. His paintings of inanimates surround us on the walls—there is a milo field at dusk, a barn wall, a barbed wire fence, a lonely windmill, an old wooden milk pail. On the floor and stuck away in corners are buckets, lanterns, a wagon wheel, old fence posts. He hands me a sheet of stationery with a Boston attorney's letterhead. "Here, Jessie, read this." I read aloud: "Your latest painting received . . . framed and hanging over our mantel opposite an original Picasso . . . very happy with it . . . evokes memories of the stark prairie in the Panhandle area . . . time seems to have stopped . . . with regards." Poe laughs heartily. "I'm hanging with a Picasso!"

Why I turned to painting, I don't know. It was a gift. I had no more desire than nothin' about painting. The only art I ever saw when I was growing up was these western magazines. I never stopped into museums or galleries when I was traveling. But the mind itself is a fantastic mechanism. What does the subconscious mind store, anyway? Maybe painting was just mulling around in my mind all the time.

All the paintings are water colors. "It's like layin' a piece of that plate glass there and hittin' it with a hammer and tryin' to guess which way it's going to break. Water colors is that way." He sprawls on a couch in the studio and begins by explaining how he started painting. He and his wife were snowed in at home. Nothing to do. He was pacing the floor. Many years before, his brother had given him some oil paints and brushes; they were stored in the closet and forgotten. "So my wife said, 'Why don't you get them oil paints out?' And that's where it started." I sit facing him in an easy chair. There is no clock in the studio. I can tell time only because the winter afternoon light dims gradually, and we are talking in semidarkness. Poe's eyes are deep inkwells. Prominent forehead ridges dominate his face. He is in his late sixties or early seventies, but he looks like a much younger man. He is hard of hearing. He initiates conversation and talks on unprompted.

When I first started out paintin', there was no way of mind to conceive how to make a composition painting, a picture. We have this big country out here, and all I could see was just a straight line: here's the sky, here's the land. That was it. No trees, no water, no nothin' else. So I just kept pecking away at it. And it looked terrible. I'd been wantin' 'em to look at the sky and the land, and all I had was just that straight horizon, and there wasn't nothin' in there of an attraction. And the colors are drab: brown and gray. We have to have a lot of rain to get some bright green grass and wildflowers. But anyway, I kept pecking away, and I knew somewhere there along that line I would find it. And you know, it just happened. I seen an old fence post, and I painted it, and I said: "Bingo. That's it!" You gotta have something for 'em to look at.

Painting now is just as hard as it was when I first started out, 'cause I'm more interested in the authentic of it. I'm more selective. I watch details pretty well. I see a lot of western paintings that have barbed wire, but they don't pay attention to the barbed wire. To me, that's the most important: the number of twists and the number of barbs.

And, of course, these cowboys we got here, they're pretty sharp. I mean, they know all the details. They got a mean eye. I painted a windmill and hung it down in the cafe here, and one of these cowboys one day, he says: "I never heard of a windmill havin' seventeen fans in it. You gotta have eighteen. Not an odd one." And I got to countin' 'em, and sure enough. That's all I had in it was seventeen.

I try to portray these people that lives here, their little castles and their barns. Nobody'd ever painted any part of this country down here. You might say everything in this part of the country's forgotten. The prairies. I paint 'em 'cause I want them to like it. I want people to know that I'm thinkin' of 'em. You know, I had an old lantern painting hanging up down at the cafe one time, and two elderly people was on the sidewalk. And they stopped and looked at that picture just for a second. And I knew all the time what they were doing. They were going back to when they had a lantern. Maybe one night there was lightning, and it struck the barn and the cow kicked the lantern over. And with a bat of an eye, just a snap of your finger, they lived a lifetime almost.

They say, "Well, why don't you paint people?" But where I'm at, there is no people. I can take you to places that's hardly been seen by a human. And there it lays, just in a perfect state, you know, like it was ten thousand years ago. I start out for my sketchin' trips, and I can go all day and never see a soul. I don't believe in isolationism, but it's just the way this country is put together. I portray it that way.

I paint buckets, lanterns, fence posts, barbed wire, windmills. Things that really exists here. Somebody was telling me that Oklahoma University made a research of what made this country hold together, and they come up with two things: windmills and barbed wire. And this is true. Windmill: you got to have water. Barbed wire: you got to have a division. This is mine, and this is yours. But I'm losing my old houses. I'm losin' my old landmarks. The new generation just pull a trailer out here. I suppose eventually it'll all be that. This is the modern age.

What motivates this idea to paint? Where do you get the ideas? You think you're going to run out of ideas, but I can walk out of this back door here of my home, and I can find a painting. It's the most exciting experience a person could have. To see it all. All at once. You set there and work with a painting, talking to each other, back and forth. And pretty soon it all begins to comin' together. It tickles me. There's a lot of things that you'll never find the answer. In painting, we can put in a dimensional form the breadth and width and the length of this rock, and we can diagnose it clear on down to the last nth. But what makes it tick? This buffalo grass. How can it lay there dormant in this arid country for so many years without some water to keep it alive? To me, it's the curiosity of nature.

I have done paintings of other locations: mountains or the ocean. But people just won't have a thing to do with it. "Poe, that's not you." They won't let me out, so my painting is still going to be just like it always has. I wouldn't trade it for anything else in the world. This little world here identifies me in an instant. But if I had to go back, I would like to paint people. These people here. You're really tested if you live in this country. It tests you for your endurance. They've been through the thick and the thin. I mean, it's a different type of a survival. Out here, you know if something fails, it's almost emptiness. But if you can just hang on, it'll get better. If I was to start over again and learn how to paint, people is all I'd do.

When I was growing up, people here were talkin' about retiring. Old age pension. And this was real frightening to me. I just couldn't believe that anybody couldn't keep on a-goin' as long as you was drawin' a breath of air. There was no such thing as retirement. And this bothered me all my life, as I was goin' through the grocery business, the meat cutting business, the real estate business, and the restaurant business. And all of a sudden, BOOM! I got a career here. So there ain't no such thing as retiring. To me, this is the most exciting thing of my life. People say, "Well, it's talent. You've got to have a certain amount of talent." And this I don't believe. I never had a paintbrush in my hand in my life till I was past forty-five. I think it's hard work. I think it's desire. You want to do it so bad. You know, I could paint with my teeth if I had to, rather than quit.

They say life's a young man's dreams and an old man's memories. I don't know. Not me. I want right now.

THE COWMEN

Quivira, city of riches! In search of its golden streets, Coronado scrabbles across the grassy buffalo land. The prairie grass is as high as a man's waist, in places as high as a man's shoulders. Coronado finds no treasure but unwittingly puts white man's footprints in county soil for the first time. The Spanish flag is inked onto maps that record his route; the Spanish crown claims the county. And the crazing legend of Quivira will not die. More conquistadors venture north; they quarrel en route, and one is murdered. The padre in the entourage condemns the murderer to eternal life in purgatory; a later party, discovering the murderer's equipment and parched bones on a

river bank, names the river *El Rio de Las Animas Perdidas en Purgatorio.*

For centuries, the cartography of greedy foreign powers has little effect on the Indians and buffalo of the prairie. Then, with suddenness, the white man's world erupts in revolution, and Mexico wrests the buffalo land from Spain. Hounded Spanish dragoons, camped on the Purgatory River, set out on a mid-winter day to hunt for food. It is bright and sunny; a warm breeze blows. That night, without warning, a blizzard sweeps in from the north. The remains of the Spaniards are discovered many years later against a cliff in the arroyo of a small canyon; the bones are wrapped in bedding, and their fingers clutch bridle reins that lead to the bones of horses.

Revolution erupts again. The rebellious child is the Republic of Texas. A new owner claims the county. Pack mules, burdened with two-hundred-pound loads of white men's cheap wares, cross the county on their way to an eager market of natives in Sante Fe. The treks across the Santa Fe Trail generate stories of Indian savagery and great profits for merchants in Independence, Missouri. Wheeled carts replace the pack mules, and their wheels mar county soil for seven score years and more. Trade continues over what is successively a portion of the State of Texas, the Territory of Kansas, the State of Colorado.

A Texas cattleman passes through in 1874 and admires the county's bountiful grasslands. With the help of uncomprehending Mexicans paid to file on several claims under different names, he acquires vast acreages and access to scarce water holes. So the JJ Ranch is born on the Picketwire River, the cowboys' corruption of the Purgatory. At one time there are ninety thousand head of JJ cattle browsing the grassy expanse of this great American steppe. The JJ brand is followed in short order, by the Box H, the T Heart, OX, 101, Rail I, FR, the Triangle Box, TH, JH9, the Half Circle L, SS, XY, the NH Triangle, the Box and Half, the Cross ML, and XX-WW.

Twice each year, in April and October, chuck wagons and cowpunchers ride out onto the range, where calves are seared with the brand of the cows they follow and are driven in relays to market or back out to pasture. Calves that go an entire season without being branded are called mavericks. The cowpunchers follow the creek beds and ride in wide circles so as not to miss any cattle, arriving at nightfall where the chuck wagons have moved during the day. It is all they can do to shovel down cold beans and lay bedrolls out in the prairie grass before surrendering to sleep, under the stars and spell of the wide prairie sky. And the cattle era, flowering, finally fixes an image on the county. The county becomes a county of cowmen, and the image persists.

Amos Bibb: Wilder Than Hell

I'm only seventy-two years old. I'm not old. I've just been here a long time.

We sit on the floor in the living room of the modest Bibb residence on the outskirts of the county seat. Amos and Lucy Bibb sit in recliners. It is an evening of warmth and fondly recounted good memories, beginning as usual with mild disclaimers. "I think you're pulling my leg," says Amos when we tell him why we've come to call. Nevertheless, limping slightly from his latest run-in with an unruly horse, he hightails it to the kitchen to pour us all bourbons. We have adapted so well to the county's Prohibitionist ethic that his offer of drink momentarily catches us by surprise. Yet, we know this man has been touted as a true old-time cowboy.

Amos expresses himself anecdotally, and Lucy vouches for every story. "Now kids, this is the truth." There are carved wood horses on the windowsill; appliquéd horses on the back of the divan; a five-foot span of longhorns on one wall, cowboy hats hung from each prong; a framed drawing of Amos riding a bronco, brands burned into the wooden frame; family photographs all about. Amos calls Lucy "Mother" or "Mommy," or, in indirect discourse, simply "her." He has craters above his temples from injuries; his fingers are long and twisted; his nose swollen; his legs bowed; and his face as wrinkled and worn as an old shoe.

I was born in Oklahoma. Born in a dugout somewhere. My dad was a cowpuncher, and when I was just a kid he went broke. In that hard winter of 1918 and 1919. When we rode over fences that winter, you didn't even know where the fences were because of the snow and ice. An' he went broke. We'd went into that winter with three thousand head, an' he came out with less than three hundred that spring. Next spring, you could walk up that canyon there for fifteen miles and never step on the ground. Step on dead cattle all the way for fifteen miles.

Hell, so I just said, "I'll just take out." So I left home when I was thirteen years old. I left home with a saddle horse and a pack horse, and I never went back home. An' I never asked nobody for a dime, from no place. I went on my own. Saddled up a horse, an' put a bedroll on another horse, and left home. I've always had a bedroll, still got a bedroll. I've got it rolled up there in the shop right now. I've had a bedroll all my life. I have led a horse and packed a bed on a horse, more miles than you can imagine, over a lot of country. An' I went back home when my dad died, and I went back home when my mother died, and that's the only times I ever went back home. I never asked 'em for a dime. Or at no place.

I met her when I was just prowlin' around over the country. I saw her out there in the yard, and I talked to her a bit, and I just got acquainted with her. An' I finally married her.

Amos and I were married in 1926. And this was like two years before the big crash on Wall Street. Actually, if we knew it, it didn't matter to us. It was something that was happening in a different world. We lived in a cow camp. I think we lived on forty dollars a month.

She was only sixteen when I married her, and I was twenty-two. An' I was wild. I didn't have a brain in my head. The only time I was happy was when I was on some buckin', crazy, fightin', pawin', kickin', runaway, fallin' horse. That's the only time I was happy. I had a wild reputation. I's wilder than hell. I was just wilder than hell. When we got married, her and I, everybody said it wouldn't last, that I was just too wild. We're gonna celebrate our fiftieth wedding anniversary just here pretty soon. But I was one of them fellows that was kind of nervous and restless. I always wanted to do something

else. I wanted to get wilder horses, meaner horses, something else. Just scatter 'round. I've stayed places long enough to have trouble with the boss, and I've had bosses didn't know which end of the cow the hay went in. But Mother, we always had a job. I could get a job on any cow outfit. All I had to do was write after 'em and tell 'em I wanted work, 'cause I was known that well. And that poor girl (Amos points at Lucy) will tell you right now. She'll admit it: we've been in cow camps where I didn't even know what color the house was. I'd leave before daylight and come in after dark.

You have to understand the ranch. In those days, ranches were big, I mean HUGE. It might be fifteen miles from the camp to headquarters. There was a headquarters. This was where either the owner or the manager lived. But he had these camps in various places over the ranch, might be fifteen miles apart. There was water but no electricity, so there was no utilities to pay; but you had this little house, you had chickens, you usually had a milk cow, and then they usually furnished meat. It wasn't a camp as such, because you had a home there. So that's a cow camp. Now this has been our life, all of our life.

She's never cussed me once. And when I've had a little money, she doesn't spend it all. She buys what she wants, and she doesn't complain. She has picked me up and hauled me in and sopped up more blood than a lot of folks ever saw, from injuries and hurts. See, I rodeoed for about eighteen years. Rode a saddle bronc. I was a saddle bronc rider. An' I was a bulldogger and a calf roper. Our life, we've had a world of fun. We've done everything, and she's been the most wonderful sport in the world.

I made a living for a long time just taking outlaw horses

and breakin' them. Breakin' outlaw horses, spoiled horses. Spoiled buckin' horses, mean horses. That was when horses meant a lot. When they had to have horses to do things with. Nowadays, I still do my work horseback. But they use more pickups. And motorcycles. But in cow country days, you didn't do it that way. When I left home, it was back in them cow country days. You could ride up and stay all night anywhere, you know. They'd feed your horse and put you up and let you stay all night.

The first place I went to work was this Flying D Bar outfit. I rode up and told 'em I was looking for a job. I was about thirteen. And this guy says, "What can you do, kid?" I said, "I can break horses." So he said, "We'll let you try, kid." And they run in a bunch of damn mares. Stuff that they didn't care anything about; you know, just a lot of horses for me to break. Well, hell, I went to forefootin' them horses, puttin' them on a stake. It was no problem. Just forefoot 'em and put a hackamore on 'em and put 'em on a stake. They thought they'd just educate me. They thought I was just a green kid and didn't know what I was doing. Hell, I broke a lot of horses.

Then I ended up at the Bell outfit. It's a big outfit, forty-two thousand cattle on the books. We pulled a wagon out on the first day of May, and we slept on the ground from the first day of May till the twenty-fourth of December. And never slept in a house. Never slept under a roof. They gave me ever' damn horse they had. And I loved it. That's just what I wanted. And they never did buck me off.

When I worked at the Cross S outfit, I stayed in camp one whole winter by myself in that little cow camp, just a little one-room cow camp. Had a little ol' fireplace, a little round Mexican fireplace in one corner. And I had my bed in the same room. And I stayed there all winter by myself. It was for a month and twenty-three days that I never saw a human in a car or at a distance on horseback or on foot. I never saw a human. There was a lot of cattle there. Hell, I was all right. I had good horses.

We never had electricity or gas in our life until 1947. Her and I went that long, and we never had electricity or gas in our life until then. It was wood. Coal, but mostly wood. It sounds like I've been through a hell of a life, but if I had to go back and do it over, I'd do it the same way. I enjoyed every bit of it. I did. It didn't bother me.

This is the thing. This is why our grandkids get such a bang out of listening to all this. It's the truth. It just happened. We never thought we had a hard life. We didn't think it was hard for Amos to get up before daylight and ride all day long. This is what a cowboy did, so it wasn't a hard life.

My daughter and grandson beat the livin' hell out of me up here in the field the other day. I was up there shovelin' 'cause we was irrigatin' this alfalfa. And they pulled in there, and I was shovelin' a little ol' place there. Hell, my back was hurtin' pretty bad, and they knew it. And they came in there and grabbed me, and my daughter got me by the shirt, and she said, "We're gonna whip you. Your back's hurtin' and you're up here workin'." But I can't . . . I can't quit. I don't intend to quit. They think I'm old, but I've just been here a long time.

THE FARMERS

Jabez Millstone was a quiet, energetic man who, at the age of thirty, got divorced, remarried, and took a long trip. It was 1885, and the marsh-drained black earth of his native Illinois was becoming too expensive for his means and too populated for his taste. Also, he could not stop imagining dubious looks and whispered conversations behind his back in town; and perhaps he was not just imagining it, because neither his first marriage nor his first wife had been above reproach. So, on June 16, 1885, Jabe packed his new wife, his two young children, his humiliation, and as much furniture as he could into a wagon, hooked up a pair of oxen, and started west.

The journey of Jabe Millstone and his family took ten months. Along its course, they pawned most of their furniture. After they crossed the Missouri, trees for firewood became so scarce Jabe was reduced to stealing roadside markers to kindle a flame for cooking the buffalo meat they purchased from mercenary skinners. One of the oxen died. On one occasion, Jabe was caught stealing a marker and fined, and he paid the fine with half a trunk of his new wife's dresses. At night, Mrs. Millstone, who hailed from Missouri, told Civil War stories to the children. She must have told them a hundred times about the time her mother put potatoes under the floorboards of their Missouri farmhouse to conceal them from the marauding Quantrill. Quantrill took their saddles and jewelry but spared their lives, and the potatoes kept them from starving. Surprisingly, somewhere on the prairie Jabe and his new wife forgot their hardships, because six months after they arrived in the county Mrs. Millstone brought forth Jabe's second son.

They arrived shortly after the terrible blizzard of 1886. The blizzard had grabbed and shaken the county like a roaring fever, at its height decimating the range stock of the large cattle companies, in its aftermath softening the ground for plowing and planting. Like hundreds of others that spring, Jabe broke out the sod and filed for a 160-acre homestead at the nearest land office, 250 miles away. He settled his family in a dugout on Wolf Arroyo, carving an open shelf into the arroyo and overlaying it with cedar logs hauled from the western part of the county and brush, grass, and spade-tamped earth. There was one window, made of oiled paper; the floor was packed earth, as were the walls. Jabe dug a well by hand and broke out ten acres to sorghum, oats, and garden vegetables. He acquired chickens, milk cows, and new oxen.

For three years, the rich, sandy loam in the county was good to Jabe, causing him to speak disdainfully of the sticky bog soil of his tiled Illinois home country. Like many farmers Jabe worshipped the sun. He planted and harvested his oats and sorghum and vegetables and weaned his calves and children by the signs. His stock and his children never were colicky, and his crops were successful. Mrs. Millstone proved as fertile as the rich, sandy loam, bearing three children in three years on the prairie, counting the boy conceived on the trip west. Jabe's long, crooked index finger was the key by which he unlocked a treasure chest of the sun's ontological secrets. When he pointed the finger at his crops, even visitors unable to grasp his animated explanations could see the glittering reflection in his eyes. "If the sun did not shine," Jabe challenged, "how would the crops grow? How would man eat? How would he survive?" His faith in the sun grew stronger with each passing day.

In 1889 the rains stopped, and they did not come again for a decade. It was a terrible time. The county emptied of suitcase farmers and many sincere homesteaders. Philadelphia mortgage companies acquired vast holdings of worthless broken sod. Town corporations folded, and townsites slowly crumbled to ruins. Jabe Millstone's faith was sorely tested. His crops did not grow, his stock died, and he was forced to hire on with a cattle company eight months of the year for wages; the other four months, ironically, he and his oldest son shamelessly preyed on stray cattle-company beeves so the family could eat.

One night, without warning, his wife complained of pain in her chest, and she tossed and moaned feverishly through the next morning. At noon, Jabe gently lifted her onto a bed of straw and blankets in his wagon and struck out eastward to search for medical help, one scrawny borrowed mule inching him along. He stopped to check his wife once after two hours and once again after three and a half hours. The second time, she was dead. The family buried her on the prairie two hundred yards from the dugout. Three weeks later, an electrical storm started a prairie fire that burned over the gravesite, and they were never sure where it was after that. No longer able to sleep well, Jabe prayed mightily all night. He prayed to the he-sun to make the she-earth produce. Sometimes he wept bitterly, but at daybreak he put on a cheerful face, even as he watched the sun rise higher and higher, ruthlessly parching his ground, day after day, month after month, year after year. In the winter, there were no storms, only flurries of light snow that the wind blew away before the thirsty earth could trap a drop of moisture. One winter morning, Jabe sent his oldest son out early to scout stray cattle-company calves. A drunken cattle-company regulator, ambitious and hungry for bounty, shot him through the eyes two miles from Wolf Arroyo. The boy had not even seen any cattle that morning. The regulator fled the county, and Jabe buried his oldest son near where he thought he had buried his wife.

Ten terrible years beat a good deal of joy out of Jabe Millstone, and he weathered into a grim, haggard receptacle of defeated dreams. Now at night he lay in half-sleep, not addressing reverent prayers to the sun that had forsaken him, but musing quiet, desultory fantasies about his Illinois childhood, his connubial shames and losses, his first few happy years on the prairie. His oldest daughter was of marrying age, and it pained him to know that, had she been exposed to schooling, a better diet, and eligible bachelors, she might have been betrothed. Yet in spite of everything, deep in his disturbed soul Jabe retained an abiding confidence that things would get better. This ineffable confidence much later came to be described as survival instinct. It was more than an instinct, but it lacked the symbolic forethought to reach the status of a philosophical conviction.

A week after Jabe Millstone's spring planting of a few acres of potatoes in 1909, heavy rains fell in the county, washing out everything. Jabe replanted. A week later the rains came again, this time lighter. Through the rest of the spring and summer, Jabe measured twenty inches of moisture by the homemade gauge he had stubbornly kept hanging on the privy door. He raised more than a ton of potatoes and, miraculously, enough volunteer grain sorghum to buy himself a milk cow. It was a good year, and then, as even today, news of good crops, cheap prices, and plentiful rainfall spread quickly through the land. The easterners rushed back into the county, many redeeming land at tax auctions, others beginning again the familiar process of homesteading. Suddenly there was talk of a railroad through the county, and speculators cranked up new town corporations on the ruins of old townsites.

Once more Jabe pointed his long, eloquent, crooked index finger at bountiful fields. When several new families homesteaded around his claim, he helped them dig wells and build dugouts in the arroyo. After a courtship of less than a year, the son of one of the new homesteaders asked for the hand of his oldest daughter. The marriage ceremony was held in a new stone schoolhouse built on the foundation of an old one a mile from Jabe's dugout. Jabe beamed through the entire ceremony, which had to be held abruptly on the chance passing-through of an itinerant preacher. After the vows, Jabe walked out of the schoolhouse and knelt on the ground. He put his lips to the rich, sandy loam and kissed it. All at once, his long, eloquent finger jerked spasmodically into the air, wildly jabbing toward the sun, and the horrified wedding guests ran to his side. His heart, albeit fortified by abiding confidence in the future, could not stand the happiness.

NEWS

1914

Winter:

REWARD $500

Whereas certain and numerous parties have been killing animals belonging to The Prairie Cattle Co., Ltd., some for the purpose of selling the meat, others for the purpose of obtaining meat for their own consumption, and others for the reason that the cattle have been giving them annoyance: This is to give notice that the above reward of $500.00 will be given to anyone giving such information as will lead to the conviction of each and every guilty party. All animals belonging to The Prairie Cattle Co., Ltd. are branded JJ on left hip, and all information should be given to Prairie Co., Ltd.

Homesteaders Ben Wills and Norland Black made proof before Judge Simpson. Dorsey Tims started his final proof notice. Amos Hellman proved up too.

Miss Opal Sherman froze her hands this morning coming to school.

Question for the debating society: Will there be any vacant land left in the county at the end of 1914?

The hens are laying.

That moisture! What are you doing to hold it?

Spring:

Dear Editor:

I think it would be best to have two or three days of fair at the county seat. Let everyone come prepared to stay for the entire fair and to exhibit their best produce, such as grain, melons, fruits, chickens, turnips, and ducks. Then, too, the ladies perhaps would like to display their fine preserves, jellies and pickles. Also cakes and breads.

Very truly yours,

Dear Editor:

It has been 26 years since we have had a fair in this county; and if we could have a fair here over a quarter of a century ago, surely we can have one now. During these past 26 years we have had some good years and some very bad ones. But take it all in all, we would be better here on our own land, than back east on someone else's land, even though our wife's people are there. A fair would be a fair way for the people to learn about the county, as they would see more in one day than they could otherwise learn in some years.

This county must have that fair. Yours truly,

Dewey Gristead had his finger torn out of its socket when he swung himself off his alfalfa load and caught his

ring (on his little finger) on a nail. He went to his house to bandage his hand and returned to find finger and ring both on the ground.

At age 65, Chuck Sampson cut a new set of teeth.

If anyone is wanting to be baptized after service next Sunday, they can be accommodated.

Dear Editor:

County fairs stimulate the energy, enterprise and intellect of people and quicken human genius. Yours,

The prospects for a crop in this county are certainly great at this time. Since Wednesday night, there has been 5½ inches of rain. This is the year for the fair.

Summer:

Dear Editor:

In our fair, we want to make a showing such as no mortal conceived to be possible in a dry country and make ourselves wonder how it was ever done. It is up to the County to give them a parade that will start the outside world singing praises of the New West in general and the County in particular. So let every neighborhood make a great float and show it at the fair! Yours sincerely,

Dear Editor:

The parade should be five miles if possible, but certainly not less than one mile. It should consist of neighborhood floats, the old soldiers division from the Spanish Civil War, troops of lads and lassies, every auto in the county and every phonograph. The fair floats should be illustrative presentations of rural scenes, like an old style school building or a weedy field. A dugout or windmill would also be suitable. Yours,

Dr. Pearl warns that the season of bowel troubles is upon us. It is necessary to boil drinking water. Make sure also to bury stools in deep holes and put in disinfectant to avoid typhoid and dysentery.

Five and one-half inches of rain fell in the last two weeks. No old timer knows of such rainfall amounts in this part of the country.

Fat and sleek antelope can be seen on the prairie.

Fall:

Dear Editor:

I wish to praise the fair and the exemplary manner in which it was conducted. Personally, I did not see evidence of intoxication. However, it is my understanding that, to some extent, this did occur. I ask you to imagine what would have happened had there been two or three saloons in town? This county has no need of saloons, and its people ought to take a shot at the wets and vote yes on the prohibitory amendment. Protect your sons from city saloons!

Yours in God,

Dear Editor:

The farmer who didn't raise good crops this year had better quit farming. I baled 101 bales of broomcorn last week. This is about 17 tons, which sells for at least $90 a ton. And I ought to have an equal value of corn, maize and cane. Is the County farming country or not?

Sincerely,

Everyone is busy, trying to take care of their bumper crop. The big harvest assures that purchasers will have money to meet their notes when they fall due.

Verle James doesn't mind cutting maize, but hates to milk the cows and get his own meals. Here's a chance for an enterprising lady!

Pioneer Tessie Herbertson, after having been taken with something like La Grippe, died after only three days of sickness. A true Christian, she was not afraid of death.

A young man got his hands on an automobile tire that didn't belong to him. As he has a good reputation, the judge told him to "Go and sin no more."

The temperature was down to zero yesterday morning but above 60 before noon. What a nice fall it has been!

1935

Winter:

SALE

I have decided to quit farming and will offer at a public sale at my farm, farm machinery, 10 head of livestock and some household goods. Lunch will be served at the noon hour.

There has been no crop for four years.

Farmers and livestock owners on relief will have feed allowances in their monthly payments to maintain two work horses, two milk cows, one hog and fifty chickens.

Cattle are being smothered. To keep cattle alive, use a stick with a long swab on it and when your cattle get so they can't breathe out of their nose, swab them.

Eating dust covered grass causes inflammation of the stomach or intestines.

God is love; God is also a consuming fire. We will reap what we have sown.

Spring:

FOR SALE

Ozark farm. No dust storms.
Electricity in house. $200 down.

A hen died of dust pneumonia.

The rabbits and squirrels are choking on blowing dust.

Teachers and janitors shovel out dust piles from the school.

The sponge supply at the county mercantile is exhausted as residents are using sponges as nose guards against the dust.

Dust comes in through keyholes in rooms.

Dead cattle have paunches filled with balls of undigested mud.

A national prayer for rain has been called. We do not hesitate to ask God for other necessities, so why not this? Kneel in prayer and join us.

The McNeil family leaves for California until the dusty weather is wetted down.

Larry Stuart is seriously ill with dust pneumonia as his lungs are dirt-clogged.

The school gym is turned into an emergency hospital to treat the many ill from dust pneumonia. The Red Cross is called in for aid.

More prayer has been offered in the past two months than in all the years since the homesteaders first came.

Two small boys, always in perfect health until the dust storms, died last week of dust pneumonia.

Little Arthur Burns (5) got frightened and turned loose of his mother's hand during a dust storm and was lost for five hours until a search party found him lying in a field.

There is not a blade of green grass or a plowed acre in the county, and everywhere is the spectre of deserted homes, barren fields, bony horses and no cattle or sheep. Farmers cannot hope for anything short of a miracle to bring them a crop in 1935.

Summer:

For Sale
Mountain ranch. Plenty of
snow and moisture here.

The crops are burning. Rain is needed.

Fall:

For Sale
New York farms for sale. No
dust and plenty of food that
livestock can eat.

Dusty weather has returned.

The county has been officially designated a drought county.

More black blizzards are predicted, even worse than last spring.

One hundred ninety-three boys arrived Tuesday for the CCC camp soil erosion program.

The WPA highway project will begin putting every relief client to work.

The county has requested federal monies for listing 250,000 acres of blow land at 50¢ an acre.

Barney, a black Percheron colt, is put to work on the Wilson Ranch. Horses, eliminated in favor of the gasoline engine, are now back because of depression prices.

Seventy-one schools open in the county: 57 one-teacher schools, 7 two-teacher schools and 7 four-year high schools. No dogs will be allowed at the schoolhouses.

There has been no moisture since June. A rainstorm would do wonders.

Farmers are hopeful for 1936.

1955

Winter:

SILAS F. YUMA:

IRRIGATION TEST HOLE DRILLING

I have drilled in this county for nine years and am familiar with all water-bearing formations here. I have just purchased special test hole equipment for this purpose.

Farmer Avis's irrigation well east of the cemetery is spurting volumes of water.

The Bryants have an irrigation well that pumps two thousand gallons of water per minute.

Crime and contest are at a minimum. The morals of our citizens are at a higher standard.

Cold blizzards but no moisture. We keep hearing reports the terrific dust storms are scheduled to begin soon.

Spring:

Dear Editor:

Although some of our narrow minded citizens are going around preaching drought, dust and hard times, irrigation pioneers Oral Bradford, Clarence Lawrence, Freeman Yokant and Delbert Delany have put down more wells. Like most old time residents, they know that with moisture, our land produces wonderful crops and with the new wells their land prices will someday double. Three cheers for those with the optimistic bug!

The Secretary of Agriculture stopped for a tour of our drought area and says that the great determination of our farmers means that the land will not be abandoned or go back to grass.

With all the rain, there might be a 60 percent wheat crop.

What a wonderful planting time with afternoon showers coming so often and bringing moisture for row crops and wheat head kernels. The buffalo grass is showing where it has not been plowed under too deep. And deep well drilling continues with farmers planning to go deeper.

Bob's Texaco Service Station will be ultra modern with window space and lights. Free cokes for all on the grand opening day!

Summer:

Notice to Parents of Boys and Girls Who Attend the V.F.W. and American Legion Dances.

I think you should go once in a while and stay in the background and just see what goes on at these dances. I think they are an incubator for Juvenile delinquency. PARENTS WAKE UP! Your Sheriff

Missing from the Steele, Walter and Bellows elevator was 120 pennies; from Clark's feed store was 3 watermelons and from Falls and Bars Store $5.00 in pennies and $6.00 in nickels.

Mr. and Mrs. Harold Brooks took the prize at the Old Settlers' Picnic for the oldest couple with a total of 155 good living years between them.

Let's find Dr. Orson some adequate housing. We have permitted some good doctors to leave for the same reason, let us keep this doctor.

Some sort of winter employment is necessary. Would a broomcorn factory be the answer now?

A gigantic neon sign spelling out MOTEL, one letter at a time, was installed at the Haven-Inn Court Motel. The rooms are very liveable.

Mr. Twiney, owner and operator of rigs for deep water irrigation wells, thinks there will be drilling done in this area for three years yet.

Fall:

Dear Sheriff:

The Veterans organizations are the only ones in the county (except the Churches) that are trying to put on any kind of entertainment for the public. So it's time to wake up and get behind the organizations that are trying to do something. THERE ARE NO ATHEISTS IN FOXHOLES.

The American Legion and V.F.W.

Broomcorn harvest is on. Wages are $7.00 a day plus board.

Shorty's cafe is sending out 180 noonday lunches daily for contractors to feed harvesters.

Big broomcorn producers Will Knute and Alva Bryant traveled last week to Oklahoma in search of harvesters. Every cabin or sleeping room is filled. Even garages are renting for sleeping. One that was rented didn't even have a door, only a canvas.

Otis Hopeland knifed Bennie Brooks, laborer at the Tommy Drew ranch. Both are from Oklahoma, here cutting broomcorn.

The restaurants are overflowing at meal time with all the harvesters. The line at the show has never been as long on Saturday night. We really need a year round industry so the harvesters can stay.

To all appearances, prosperity is just around the corner for this area.

Mrs. Green: Then the Wind, I Loved It

Mary and Max Green live in a ramshackle frame house on the prairie. It was built in 1916, half a mile from where Max's father homesteaded in 1885. To the Greens' seven children, twenty-five grandchildren, and eleven great-grandchildren, it is still known as "the old home place." On the wall in the dining room is a large framed photograph of the Navy destroyer that Al the Cowman, the Greens' oldest son, rode for twenty-six months during World War II.

As we unpack our tape recording equipment, Mr. Green advises his wife to be careful. "They're going to turn that thing on," he warns. Mrs. Green announces she has no intention of talking. "You're the old farmer," she reminds Max. Five minutes later, both begin to recount long family histories. Mrs. Green interrupts her husband frequently and mercilessly. She grows impatient with his deliberation and understatement. Eventually, she completely takes over the conversation. The first interview lasts several hours; it is followed by many others.

I think that what I remember more about this country was the first impression I ever had. When we came here in

1914, we came in a covered wagon. And they had more rain than they had ever had before or since. It was completely covered with wild flowers: gladioluses, only we called them nigger heads; and then wild honeysuckle. Oh, there was all kinds of flowers. And it was just like that as far as you could see. There was houses, but mostly little dugouts or just small houses and a small patch of farmed land around them. Twenty acres would have been a big patch for anybody to have worked. And there was no fences. It was just completely open prairie, just as far as you could see.

And I remember that wind. I used to love that wind. But you see, there was no dirt because it was all prairie. Grass. The wind could blow, but there was no dirt. And us kids used to like to run in the wind, and we'd hunt buffalo horns and arrowheads. I remember I had long hair, and I don't know why they'd do it, but my brothers, they'd make me unbraid my hair. They'd coax me to, and then I'd run, and I was supposed to be a sailship and that was the sail. My hair was a sail. And then they'd try to catch me. My two brothers were younger and I could outrun them, and they'd holler about the sailboat. And we'd play for hours that way. "Here comes the sailboat." But the wind. Then I loved it.

She recalls water fights with her mother in the old horse tank and the nickel rewards she earned for washing her father's feet. She remembers hard winters when the neighbors' horses ate the shingles off their roof and still starved to death. And the spring thaw that allowed her father to travel around the countryside, skinning the hides off of dead cattle, still partly frozen from the long winter frost.

People had their fears. If the grass got dry, there was a chance a prairie fire might start any time. There was no

stoppin' it hardly; they just took everything in front of 'em. It was just an inferno. And everybody that could see the fire'd take barrels of water and gunny sacks and brooms to help fight it. When my father'd go to get the freight, it would take two days and a night, and my mother couldn't rest for being so afraid of prairie fires. She'd just walk the yard and look. She didn't get over it until after the country was broke up.

After they broke it up for wheat in the twenties, that ended that. In the twenties, the eastern farmers come here, suitcase farmers, we called 'em. They plowed up the sod. It was profitable. And then we had no more than got that land into production than the drought hit; and then instead of having prairie fires, we had dirt storms. A prairie fire, the grass'd come back prettier the next spring than it was before. That dust bowl: it ruined farming completely.

Everybody that's been in this country very long can tell you about the dust bowl. We had dirt blow from '32 till along about '39 or '40. The old-timers always have a joke: it's normal when it's dry, and the abnormal years was when it rained. We had what they call rollers: those old, dark, black clouds of just pure dirt. And when you took that out, you took it out with a scoop shovel.

I don't know. In a way it was good for people. It cemented friendships. Their houses was all just blowing away, and their crops were gone, and they were all hard up. We used to just make a half of a day visiting when we'd take the cream to town to sell. Well, just as soon as they got more prosperous, they had big new cars and this, that, and the other. They quit visiting. I think you need a little bit of shaking up every so often. We forget. 'Cause nature is the boss.

"Hi, Jessie." Mrs. Green greets me in the driveway, where six or seven vehicles are parked, some temporarily, some for the last dozen years. She wears a light blue housedress that barely covers her close-to-the-ground bulk. It is early, and she has not done her toilet. Her gums are as empty as a baby's, and her long hair (white at the scalp, black at the waist) has not been twisted into the tight bun she usually wears. We stroll along walkways stamped into the dirt by years of colonization at the old home place: a bungalow occupied by her youngest daughter and her family; a renovated old shed inhabited by one of the grandsons and his wife; a clearing reserved for another

grandson who intends to move in a trailer when he marries in a month; a huge vegetable garden where Mrs. Green pauses to tug at some weeds. South of houses and barns and shops, we come to the hog-growing facility operated by Tom, one of the grandsons. We pause at a small A-framed farrowing hut. A massive, flesh-colored sow lies on the ground, panting quietly. She has just given birth, and her pug nose twitches sporadically as a spray device blows a fine vapor mist into the hut. Her babies suckle eagerly at her long teats. Tom walks over and explains that the heat may have curdled her milk; she doesn't seem to be producing enough. He reaches down and retrieves the three-pound runt of the litter and pulls a baby bottle from his pocket. Mrs. Green cradles the helpless little pig, tucks the bottle in its mouth, and it drinks contentedly. Mrs. Green smiles a toothless, happy smile.

You will never know what a terrible agony it was. I had a baby in the middle of a dust storm. On that particular day, the doctor decided to run off with the schoolteacher. The baby weighed two and a half pounds when he was three weeks old. And he had no doctor. We had to put up sacks at the windows to hold the dirt off him. He could not have breathed the air that we had.

We made what we called an incubator out of pasteboard boxes. And we put bricks and flatirons between the boxes to keep him warm. The first time I ever saw him, he'd lay too long on one side of his head, and it had caused it to cave in. I thought some of my little kids had hit him. Well, I turned him over, and then his head filled in. Then I knew what that was. It was because I left him lay too long. I fed him with a medicine dropper.

Finally, my husband found this doctor, and he said, "Well, I'm going to tell you. There ain't a damn bit use of you trying to raise that kid because you can't do it." And he said, "You just as well forget it before she gets attached to him." (She laughs.) Well, I was attached to him from the beginning. So this child never had any doctoring. Now we tease him about being the fattest.

My kids don't think they had hard times. I don't think they ever knew. I've asked them, and they say, "We didn't know we was poor." I remember one time, it come Thanksgiving Day, and I didn't have anything to cook but some beans, and I didn't have any fire to cook 'em with because we'd run out of fuel. Had to have gas for the stove. So I told the kids to help me pick up some cow chips and some sticks and build a fire on a stove in an old well house we had. So we got the stove to goin', and I baked light bread and cooked those beans on there. Well, the kids was out playing, and when I finally got 'em done it was gettin' kinda late. It was Thanksgiving Day, and I bawled like a fool 'cause I thought, "Oh dear, Thanksgiving and no pumpkin pie. Just them beans." Well, finally got 'em ready to serve to the kids. Carried 'em back in the house. Called 'em, and Al, my oldest, come in the door. He said, "Oh, kids. Goody, goody. Ma's got beans and hot bread." And do you know, I never felt better like I did then? My kids were just completely happy.

Sunday mornings, Mrs. Green gets in the old dusty Falcon sedan her father bought just a few months before he died and navigates the thirty-five miles of county dirt roads and oiled blacktop to the county seat. She attends a nondenominational prayer service in the private home of a fellow worshipper. The service is led by a pair of itinerant preachers they call the "Two-by-Twos," men and women who travel from town to town preaching the Gospel the way He intended. After the service, Mrs. Green begins the long journey back, stopping along the way to visit the six of her seven children who do not live at the old home place. "My husband's so old-fashioned, he don't want to be moving around. I could have a lot of fun going to see the kids if he'd go along, but I go to see them alone. He don't like to leave this farm. He said he was born here, and when he left, he'd be in a box." Just before dark, she completes the last inspection. Her brood intact, she returns to Max and the farm.

The Lord sends rain on the just and the unjust. I don't think it was God trying to punish. It was just time to have a dust bowl. Cycles of moisture and cycles of drought. It was just part of the ways of the moon and the sun and the stars and the way that the universe is set up.

When I was a kid, I used to worry about how long the world was going to last. People used to just constantly talk about the world coming to an end. I used to think just little sins, just kind of ordinary misdemeanors, was enough to send you to hell. And I grew up believing that we can make our own destiny. I thought that if I didn't do just exactly right, that I'd be punished by my children being taken. I don't believe that now. The children of the very best people, they're all going to suffer the same. They could have accidents, or they could be taken. We've got to learn to accept whatever comes and not to feel like that it would be sent on us for punishment. My nature would make me want to feel guilty whether I was or not. And I don't suppose anybody ever does the very best they can. And sometimes your best isn't the right thing to do.

The screen door on the back sun porch slams shut, and a teen-age grandson brushes through the dining room and heads wordlessly for the bathroom. A granddaughter is drying dishes in the adjoining kitchen. "Remember, Jean," Mrs. Green lectures, "beauty is as beauty does." Jean nods, puts down the dish towel and accepts a hug from her grandmother. Sylvia, Mrs. Green's resident adult daughter, her youngest, comes in the back door with news that there's been a false fire alarm at the hospital in town. Mrs. Green goes directly to the telephone and calls her daughter-in-law, the one who lives across the street from the hospital. "Watch that kid of yours," she counsels. "He's one for mischief." The screen door slams again. It's another grandson come to visit, Al the Cowman's oldest son, a lanky twenty-seven-year-old. Al Junior heads for the bathroom and tries the door.

"Andy," Mrs. Green calls to the teen-age grandson who has not yet emerged. "Al Junior wants in." Al Junior waits in a deep easy chair. Mrs. Green asks about Al Senior. She wishes he wasn't into cattle so heavily. She also worries out loud about her youngest son, a leading spokesman for the American Agriculture Movement. Rumor has it he wants to relocate to more clement surroundings. Al Junior tries to reassure her. "He's just blowing." Mrs. Green won't be reassured. "It ain't right. He just can't sell out and leave the others." She is thinking of all the joint business ventures her five sons have built up: dryland farms, irrigated farms, feedlots, farm supply stores, grass ranches. "Besides, there's no place that has better soil than we have here, if we can just get the moisture. Why, I wouldn't give this up for anything."

Sometimes I think we don't want a will. This lawyer said my husband shall will everything to me and I will everything to him, so we can dispose of it in any manner we want. Whichever one shall be the survivor. Well, I said to my husband, "Max, for heaven's sake, I'm not going to sign such a will as that." And he said, "Why?" And I said, "Why, you can get married to some old floozy the next day, and she would just have half the property." (She laughs.) I really don't know. He said that he would never live by himself, and when you get to be seventy years old, somebody that comes along that wants to take care of you might not be very desirable. I don't know. See, both our fathers worked their life away just to have land to leave to their children. And we got our share of the land. It's all been worked hard to get, and I sure wouldn't want to divide it with no second wife or second husband, either one. To me, I just see his dad and my dad wanting land for the kids. That's all you ever heard out of my father or his father, either one. "Lay up land for the children."

I think any good farmer, anybody that sticks with it, has to love the land. Has to feel a part of the earth. If you didn't like the ground, you couldn't go out here and grow anything. When you sow that seed, you got to know just how to put it in there, and you've got to feel like it's going to come. And if you don't get it the first time, you've got to try again. That's farming. You just keep trying. And then you live on hope.

2 ☙ *Around Town*

I remember years back. Transportation wasn't as fast as it is now or anything, but more people would get together and they'd be a whole community together. Visit and enjoy themselves. You don't see that anymore, sure don't. You go over and help your neighbor, he asks how much he owes you. Everyone's chasing the nickel.

A county old-timer

I hate not being able to slip anonymously into a supermarket, lost in my thoughts, fantasies, daydreams, to cruise the aisles without being offered help over and over again, to pick out as little as I want without feeling I'm being observed and spending too little, to buy all the chicken I want without feeling I'm a traitor to beef country, and to carry my own bags without feeling guilty about the grocer toting them down the block if I've been stupid enough to park far away. I am suffocating from community. I will not eat.

Jessica's diary

BREAKFAST

Seven o'clock in the morning. It could be slightly earlier or later, depending on the weather and the time of year. The key: sunup. Down at the Hitching Post the regulars arrive one by one, filling up the six chairs and the five window-seat places at the big head table by the east window, in front of the cash register, the Skoal and beef jerky rack. Here, Al Green, the cowman, holds court seven days a week, rain or shine; and here, their prerogatives to speak and joke (not to mention their very right to sit) finely regulated by age and family lines, the regulars conduct the major business of the world, their world, with an enviable lack of accountability and a healthy measure of hindsight. The head table is commonly called the liars' table. Late-coming regulars are forced to find seats over near the coffee pot or in booths back by the restrooms, where they share tabletops and mutually uninvigorating conversation with laborers and hired hands and unpedigreed bachelors, too far from the head table to hear anything but the laughter when Al the Cowman scores with a yarn or a witty retort. (In harvest season, the custom crews on tour trickle in for two or three hours each morning, unshaven, wearing tattered coveralls and seed caps, instinctively and circumspectly moving to the back booths as far away as possible from the liars' table.)

There is a rule: while the regulars may cross the line from the head table to the booths and smaller tables, the crossing rights are not reciprocal. There are exceptions, however, people like Moon Jackson and his brother Peewee; Peewee because of the honor accorded septuagenarians, Moon because of the grudging respect his bad reputation has won him among the regulars, most of whom believe themselves a better class of people. The regulars know that had Moon not fallen from grace twenty years ago, had that one moment of raging passion not robbed him of five years of freedom and his life's stock of achievements, it might be Moon Jackson, not Al the Cowman, holding court at the liars' table today.

The regulars defined: predominantly older cowmen and farmers in their fifties and sixties, men of the allodial establishment with sons taking over, and a few of the agribusiness proprietors who, were they not present every morning, might suffer serious rather than playful derogation of their seeds, their fertilizers, their combines, their pump engines.

Physiognomy and dress: Al the Cowman—large, wide-brimmed cowman's cowboy hat (straw in summer, brown felt in winter), tall and slim-hipped but (occupational disability) watermelon-bellied, weathered handsome face marred by snuff-stained teeth, faded Levis, faded western shirt, scuffy cowboy boots, and always the big silver belt buckle with the home-place brand X/X. His partner and ubiquitous companion, Tex, cowman and land trader—short of stature, truly blessed with the smile and looks of a western movie star (many a good trade has closed on these blessings), salt-and-pepper cropped hair, attired in crisp Levis and conservative cowboy hats and shirts. Buford, the biggest landowner in the county—always got up like a pauper farmer, red-complected, paunchy, smile as ready and honest as high mountain brook water, blond hair whitening attractively with age, every day the same blue cap with the Chevrolet emblem, the same sorry rundown cowboy boots. The tractor-pulling hobbyist Sam—hatless as always, swarthy mellow face, thinning gray hair, partial to blue shirts. Norland, the pump man and cattle speculator—fancy boots and clean pair of boot-cut Levis every day, fashionably uncountrified longish hair, no hat. His older brother, Ernie—big farmer, chain smoker, nervous hands and eyes, end joint of right index finger missing, his cowman getup a shade more slovenly than anyone else's. Then, always, Peewee, who spends his days sitting in front of the variety store in his old white pickup—large bulbous nose, weathered traces of Indian in his face, sad eyes, pock-marked, a belly so huge he must shuffle cautiously to be sure of the ground in front of him, the same sweat-stained cowboy hat for all seasons; a fixture, never spoken to, ignored, ordering coffee morning after morning, spooning ice into it from his water glass and slurping up the tepid brew between drags of unfiltered Chesterfields all the way down to his fingertips. And, only sometimes, for he arrives and leaves earlier than most of the other regulars, Moon, Peewee's younger brother—same sad eyes, same nose and pock marks, smaller belly, voluntarily but unfailingly dressed in prison-gray matching work

shirt and pants (Can he never forget those five years? Does he want to remember them?), comical gray cap with gray leather bill; also ignored and not spoken to, but a big eater, appetite commensurate with his harsh daily regimen, long hours lifting pipe and welding, long evenings spent alone.

And the others, variants on common themes: a medley of cowboy hats, seed caps, coveralls, Levis, brown and gray work pants, cowboy boots, ruddy and swarthy complexions inked into rugged facial topography, work-swollen thick and stubby hands and fingers, scars, grease, grime, scabs, bruises, overhanging bellies, city-office white foreheads from hat-brim sunscreening, shirt pockets bulging with checkbooks, pencils, canisters of snuff, cigarettes, seed company handouts, Alka Seltzer tabs, and capsules for high blood pressure.

The Hitching Post is on the state highway north of town. Sis acquired it back in the Depression in return for cancellation of a promissory note she held. One day many years after the Depression, Al the Cowman had some of his boys at the feedlot paint up a big wooden sign, which they hung over the Hitching Post door late at night. The sign read: THE HAWG TROFF. Although Sis took the sign in stride, six months later she sold out. Nobody said Al the Cowman's sign did it, but the fact was that Sis had been trying to unload the cafe for decades. Her buyer was a guy from Ohio who worked on a dairy farm as a kid; that didn't prepare him for cow country.

Guys eat the same thing every morning. They'll eat the same thing. Of all the people I've ever been associated with, I've never seen anything like it. The cake and egg is a good one. Sausage is good. We serve more sausage with breakfast than any other meat. I'd say more sausage than ham and bacon put together. Sausage and two eggs, hash browns, I'd say is our biggest breakfast. And they like pancakes just the opposite of the way you get in the city. They want 'em big around, and thin. Thin as you can get 'em. And Dutch honey syrup. That's hard to make. Hard to find. You've got to have fresh cream from a cow that's never had anything done to it. It's illegal if you ever get caught serving it. It's just pancake syrup, cream, and sugar. I'm not allowed to buy this cream. The fact is, I don't even know the person that sells it to me. I've never seen him.

Conversation: problems with the corn borer in minimum tillage planting; good trades on new pickups or used tool bars at a farm auction; "Gunsmoke"; the last high school varsity game; prices; weather.

Sam the tractor-pulling enthusiast has cake and egg every morning. Buford the big landowner has cake and egg in the summer, a bowl of hot oats and four teaspoons of sugar and a glass of milk when the weather turns cold. Al the Cowman drink coffee. Tex is another cake-and-egg man. One large doughy pancake, burnt in spots, overhanging the plate. One egg over-easy on a side dish. Margarine tabs and Dutch honey syrup in the center of the table. Styles differ. Tex puts his egg on top of the syrupy cake and mashes it up, then salts and peppers the mash. Sam wolfs down most of his cake, then eats his egg with the last three bites of cake and syrup. Buford puts on margarine and syrup, cuts the cake in half, folds the halves together, pours on more syrup, then puts the egg on the cake plate in the half left over after the folding operation.

Got your trucks ready? Al the Cowman's youngest brother runs an implement store and, as a sideline, hauls

cattle. One load? Yeah; got some fats I want to get killed by tomorrow. Be ready. By God, I tell ya, these damn prices come back up I'm agonna cut loose from this cow business. Hell, you'll just start expanding. Laughter.

Sold any land lately to pay for that damn habit? tractor-pulling Sam is kidded. Laughter. I heard them corn borers survive real good over the winter in that wheat stubble. I got the bore worse than any you fellas. No, says Tex, there's others got it worse. Who? (Tex points at himself while chewing a mouthful of cake and egg.) Laughter. What happened to that old red pickup of yours? Bearing out. That's what you get ownin' them Fords. Laughter. Ain't you glad you got a Chevy, Buford? Goin' down to Oklahoma to trade on a new Ford pickup today. Don't you trade local no more? Sheeee. . . .

Sam the tractor-puller tells a joke: How many animals fit in a pair of panty hose? Ten little piggies, two calves, a pussy, and God knows how many hares. Laughter. Allis and John Deere are popular, their shortcomings solicitously analyzed for days. Internationals take abuse. Get you one of them green machines, wouldn't be runnin' after parts all the time. Damn sure right. Sam has another one: How come women can't judge distance? The answer: All their lives, they've been told this (holding up hand with thumb and forefinger an inch apart) is nine inches long. Laughter. Genealogy stories. Now what was his name? Had a brother name of Wiley, lived over there west of Austin's place. Old Man Robinson died last night. Quite a fighter. Don't you reckon, Tex? Say he bit ole Bacon Rind's ear off. They got into it over something. That damn fence there up north, wasn't it? Anyway, doctor come out there, wanted to sew that sonovabitchin' ear back on. Old Man Robinson, though, he swallered it. Oh, he'd give a man a thumpin'. Fella'd bring one of them daughters back late, be out there with that ole shotgun. Eighty-seven years old, an' keener 'n hair on a frog's back.

I tell ya, this damn cattle deal. Rained out east. What'd ya get? Forty-hundredths. Drier'n a sonovabitch up north. Goddamn. Down to Oklahoma buyin' some of them Okie steers. Just not too goddamn bad. A fella winter 'em on some corn stalks up here, have some pretty damn sleek sonovabitches come spring. You trade down there? Now, you ain't kiddin'. Four hundred head. Count 'em? Now, goddamn right I did. They didn't run 'em 'round the hill on you? Laughter.

Pay up. Hell, a man shouldn't oughta put no money on Oakland. Hell, the Vikings. Sheeeee. Buncha damn niggers jus' throwin' them white boys around. BIG ole niggers, too! What'd ya get down south? Thirty-hundredths. Damn, I guess I jus' ain't livin' right. Who's farmin' that out east now? Oh, some damn trust outfit. Damn sure gonna save a fella buncha taxes. Hell, no, I didn't plant no sweet corn. Fed the whole damn county last year. You too? Sheeee. . . .

In groups of two and three, they pay out and leave, mounting pickups to drive to the fields, working two-way radios as they go, arms and shoulders hunched over steering wheels to make it easier to wave to passing drivers. By eight most of the regulars are gone, although a close basketball game the night before may require replaying clear to nine o'clock, and a bit of dew during harvest will keep everybody in until the sun's high in the sky. After they've checked their operations, they'll trickle back in to coffee for a spell in the middle of the morning; and then they may be joined by the likes of the gas man and the full-time town employees, the contemptible class of locals who have never really put in an honest day's work in their lives, never experienced the crushing weight of debt, never bought anything bigger than a car or a house. Peewee, of course, will hang around till ten-thirty, when the mail's up, then get into his white pickup, drive half a block to Main Street, and park in front of the variety store. If he's lucky, he'll get a social security check.

At eleven-thirty, they'll begin to come in for dinner, the make-up of the group somewhat altered by the added presence of farmers and cowmen from out in the country who can't afford to take time off from chores in the morning. Moon Jackson will also be among the first in for dinner, among the first out again to grapple with the eternal certainty of dull manual labor until darkness, his wages of sin the wages of a hired man who could have been something better.

Boy, it's different than from where I come from. Chicken fry. I never heard of it before. I can't say that I like it. We must serve twenty-five or thirty chicken fry dinners a day. I just can't say that's a good piece of meat. To me. And where I come from, if you made a bean dinner like we make a bean dinner, you wouldn't sell none. You use pinto beans, you wouldn't sell none. Same way with putting 'em in chili. They wouldn't buy that back home. Make your chicken fry with your cube steak or your minute steak. Breaded. Like you would a veal cutlet. In fact, take the same piece of meat: if it's veal cutlet, put brown gravy on it, and if it's chicken fry, put white gravy on it. But I tell you, I've never seen anything like it. These guys'll set over here and spend five or six hours a day in here talking about how hard they work. They just act like they don't like home life. And they manage three meals a day in here. Every day. Just like they don't want to go home.

This is a man's world. It is the same world, day after day, year after year, generation after generation. Cake and egg, chicken fry, coffee, sausage, water-glass ice in coffee, tradition, habit, constancy.

Moon Jackson: Five Years of My Life

I am cleaning out the parts supply garage on Main Street, which will soon be the town's first law office. A battered blue Chevy pickup pulls in; there are racks of propane tanks and rows of metal tubing in the bed. Moon Jackson clambers out. He is wearing gray work clothes. "You the new lawyer?" he asks in his mild, gentle voice. Word travels fast. Moon wants me to represent him in county court on a traffic offense: driving under the influence. It is not his first DUI. As a result, if convicted, he faces revocation of his license and a mandatory jail term. I don't like traffics, but I reluctantly embrace a live client.

Word travels fast. The town policeman stops by to tell me how belligerent Moon was the night the citation was issued. "Had to radio over to the county seat for the sheriff and a deputy to restrain the subject." At the cafe, after Moon has departed of a morning, some of the allodial ones tell me to watch out. Moon's done some terrible things. Much is left to the imagination. I spend several hours preparing a case for trial. There is a defect in the citation, and I stroke the deputy D.A. Eventually we make a deal, and Moon is pleaded to a lesser offense. He keeps his license, pays the county a fifteen-dollar fine, and does not go to jail. It takes me several months to get up nerve to try to interview him, but eventually we become first-name friends: he calls me Jeff, and I call him Mr. Jackson. He has not touched hooch since the night he got that DUI. He carries the key to the county A.A. meetings and makes the A.A. coffee.

I came back 'cause I was raised here. I was born in this country. Daddy homesteaded in 1911. I was born down south there on Wolf Arroyo. Born in 1917. This is my country, and I'm gonna stay.

Daddy owned a pool hall and a picture show down south. Silent pictures. Had the pool hall and candy and stuff. He run that, and then it burnt down. But he never did build back. Just left it. Stayed there on the farm and farmed. Then he bought a hotel. Then the railroad come through up here in '26, an' they moved that whole town down south up here where we are now. Pulled that hotel up here on a horse trailer along with everything else. I remember that: that whole town. Eight or ten horses pullin' each house . . . on dollies, steel dollies, and big wide tires. Then we moved up here. I can remember when we first come up here. Before the first outside privy was here. Right there where the Texaco station is at.

Watching television in Moon's living room: overflowing ashtrays, bare wood floors, mismatching sofa and chair, a big picture frame with two photographs under glass ("I got the frame at an auction for a dollar"). He shows off the stockpile of horseshoes and hames in his basement, the raw material from which he welds artful tables and ashtray holders for people to buy at Christmas. He has just bought another old pickup, and this one he's going to convert into a coyote wagon. He explains with childlike pride how he's got in mind a coyote skinner made out of some old well casing and a stretcher. Each pelt brings twenty-five dollars. A man can make a lot of money. Whenever I stop by at night, the blue light of the television inside is visible from the street. Moon watches a lot of television.

Well, I can remember when we set around on those old streets here in town with all that booze. And it was the ol' cowman. There wasn't no law, you know. They didn't have no paved streets, no sidewalks or nothin'. Just buildings. It was just dirt streets, and they had old Model Ts. Some of 'em rode horseback in. If you had to go to the grocery store, you just kinda slid down in it. I can remember goin' in there. One time, I went in with the folks. They had this coconut in barrels, wooden barrels. Might be, you know, shredded coconut. Ol' cat had kittens on this coconut in there. Hell, the ol' boy that run it just dipped the top of it. Went right ahead and selled it. Well, they wasn't nobody knew it, you know. I guess as long as they didn't know it, they wouldn't hurt none.

Then they finally went on and got some sidewalks. They raised a lot of broomcorn then. That started along in the late thirties, I'd say. I s'pose wages then was anywhere from a dollar to a dollar and a half a day. And board and room. I've seen these streets so full of people during broomcorn harvest that you couldn't get to the grocery store. You'd have to go down the middle of the street and cut in. There'd be that many people. And they fought. They killed each other. I don't know how many was killed. Fights after fights with them Indians. Indian's worse in the world, I guess, when he gets drinkin'. Saturday nights was terrible. Saturday and Sunday.

Then times started gettin' better, and the town improved a little. You know, built streets a little better an'

sidewalks an' some newer buildings. 'Course there in the thirties, when we'd have those dirt storms, why, there wasn't anything you could do anyway. I saw 'em roll in here, oh, you'd just pretty near have to look straight up to see the top of 'em. It'd just be like a black cloud. It was rollin', and ever' kinda bird in the world would be right ahead of it, see?

When I met my wife, I was runnin' them dances here in town. That was in the thirties. Had dances ever' Saturday night. I think we charged fifty cents to get in. But I drew people from all over the country. Hell, we danced in dirt storms and everything else. The only reason they didn't come'd be because they couldn't see to get here. But I never will forget. One couple. They got pretty loaded, and they'd dance, and they fell and kinda rolled around there a little on the floor. Gettin' up, you know, about half drunk. Her dress kinda come up, and she had a pair of pants on that said "Diamond M." They had flour then that come in a Diamond M flour sack. She'd made a pair of pants out of it. But I never will forget that. It had that Diamond M right on it.

Me and my wife met there. At the dance. We went together quite a while. She was six years younger than me. Got married in '38. Raised five kids. 'Course, I've been divorced since '53. Really don't care whether I ever see her again or not. Cost me three years and twelve days. I actually done that much time. That was what that divorce deal cost me.

One day, these friends come by, and they was goin' shoppin' up north. And we had kids, and I told my wife, well, I'd stay with the kids while she went up to do some shoppin'. Well, she didn't come home. And along about after dark, along come my mother to stay with the kids. And I had a new DeSoto car. And I just went up there. I had a pretty good idea what the deal was, you know. And I just went up to that townhouse there and parked this car around behind it. Went and looked in the window. She had a nice lookin' soldier boy. I set out there a while and watched. They went to the car. Drinkin', and I s'pose screwin' too. I don't know. Hell, I just got in the car and come on home. And it was gettin' late when I got home, so I took off my clothes and went to bed. But never did go to sleep. And she come in about four o'clock in the morning. I asked her where she'd been. She told a big lie about it, see? 'Cause I'd already saw her. (He pauses.) Well, I beat her about half to death. I was mad. I wouldn't hurt her now again. But I put her in the hospital a couple of weeks. And that's when this divorce deal come up.

They got me for nonsupport. You didn't have a chance, you know. I probably spent two thousand dollars. Hired a lawyer, but they wasn't a damn thing you could do. It was all set up. You just didn't have a chance. I s'pose, the time I was there, a good many of 'em was there for that. Pretty near all of us was there for some little thing like that. I tried to set up a fund for the kids, to buy clothes and things. And they said I was gonna have to give the money to her. I said, "By God, I won't." And I never. I never would. I'da stayed away from then till now if I coulda. You just didn't have a chance, you know. That was the deal on that.

They took about five years of my life. On parole and the time I was runnin'. It took 'em a year to catch me. Just things like that. I went to old Mexico. Up and down the border. Arizona, Texas. Anywhere a freight train went, I went. That's the only way you could stay away from 'em. I stayed off down in there, me and this old boy together. This old boy was real educated. He'd been all over the world. Kinda showed me the ropes. We buddied up. We'd find a boxcar with some straw. Just get in there and go to sleep, and wherever it ended up, that's where you was at. Once down in Kansas City, we hired out for the Salvation Army. They paid so much, and then you got your meals, your room. You go out on these trucks. We'd climb on those trucks, gatherin' up all the stuff all over Kansas City. An' we had us an apartment rented downtown. (He laughs.) My buddy drove the truck. If we's lucky, about half a load, we'd go through that stuff and get anything we wanted. I had several pairs of slippers, you know. I had a new one for every day of the week. Coats for every day of the week. He did too. And we'd store this stuff in that apartment house. We had four or five suitcases apiece. But we had some of the fanciest suits you ever saw. We'd change color every day. (He laughs.) I don't know what I ever did do with 'em. Socks, too, lots of socks. But we made a lot of money. Got around to all these rich areas, when people'd buy new furniture. Long divans. And they had a big dock out there, and we'd set these divans out there on that dock. We'd wait for everything to close up, and then we'd come in there, take a pocketknife and slit that divan to the bottom on the back. Just rip 'er open. And we found higher than ten dollars worth of change right there. Quarters, half dollars. Lost out of them rich folks' pockets. They started wonderin' what happened to all them divans.

But finally I got caught. We was workin' in Kansas, plannin' to go up to Chicago. I really wanted to go. I wanted to see Chicago. We was stayin' in a hotel. Had a couple of gals. Asked the porter to bring somethin' to drink, you know. He come to the door and knocked. It was kinda late, and I went to the door. And it was the goddamned FBI. They caught up with me, see? They'd been lookin' for me, but it took 'em a year to do it, see? He told me, he said he'd been awful close a few times. But I'd lost him. Well, they had a real hard time catchin' me. I hope they did. They could get within two, maybe three weeks of me, but you get on a train, they don't know where to find you.

After I got out, I come back here and got straightened up. Come back here and went to work. I still think this is probably as good place as they are for a poor man to start. Just start with nothin'. I had owned a farm. Owned lots of machinery. I lost it all, see? That's one of the things that'll happen to you. Three or four years up there. I went to work for farmers. Drove a tractor. Work for wages and room and board for some farmer. Sharecrop with him. If you was lucky and had a pretty good crop, you had a little steak. But I got to drinkin' a lot. That done me more damage than anything. It takes you a long time to live something like that down, you know. I know people, I don't s'pose ever will forget it. Some of 'em don't want to. I think some of 'em would want to keep hearin' it, you know. Them people never done me no good anyway.

I have a lot of friends that come by, you know. People that knew me real good. But you've got a certain class of people, they'll just believe anything.

It is Christmas time, and some of the "young adults" from the First Baptist Church, where we have been attending, have been trying to track us down to go caroling with them. Jessica is out of town, as it happens, and I am riding around with Moon Jackson in his coyote wagon. At dusk he drops me off at the law office to pick up my car. Next door at the First Baptist Church some of the young adults watch as Moon and I stand for a few moments in the fading light and talk about guns and coyotes. When Moon drives off, a young woman strides over and asks if I can go caroling. I beg off because of other obliga-

tions. "Was that Moon Jackson you was with?" she asks. I say yes. She shakes her head. "I thought so." She tells me Moon is not somebody to hang around with.

You know how it is. Some people's that-a-way. All my life, they ain't done me no good. It's just a class of people that was raised here. And I've probably spent more money in my life than they've earned. But you couldn't get enough off of 'em to buy a pack of cigarettes. I've worked as hard as any of 'em. You can ask anybody that's been here. I used to cut broomcorn. There never was a man could outcut me in a broomcorn field. There's never been one. There might now, 'cause I've got too old. But there never was a man. Back when times was hard, you'd pay 'em a dollar a day to cut broomcorn. Wherever I worked I drew a double wage.

When I was married, I didn't drink. Except for dances or parties, like anybody. This divorce deal, I couldn't stand that. But I don't think about it anymore. It was a hell of an experience, not a very good one; and it could've been worse. But still, five years out of my life. I always thought some time or other they'd make that unconstitutional. I'd like to have sued 'em for that. But there ain't no way. They just took about five years of my life.

MAIN STREET

The big Bartlett elevators stand across the street from the cafe, beside the state highway that parallels the tracks at the north end of town. East of the elevators, fringing both sides of the state highway for the rest of its easterly path through town, is a continuous jumble of refuse and dying enterprise. There are three filling stations, an abandoned railway station, rusted oil and gasoline storage tanks, two abandoned metal elevators, a broomcorn warehouse, nondescript sheds, propane tanks, the Cash Co-Op elevator complex, the Allis-Chalmer dealership, and a fertilizer depot. In the interstices of the jumble, custom cutters berth their combines and grain trucks during harvest and, after harvest, the two functioning elevators pile up mountains of sugar beets, wheat, and milo—overflow from the bins, silos, and roundtops. North of the tracks is the airport, a graded swath through a cow pasture; the local aerial sprayer and three well-heeled irrigation farmers keep their single-engine light planes in individual corrugated steel hangars. A dentist from a hundred miles away risks the winds, the tallest Bartlett elevator, and the pitted runway every other Tuesday afternoon.

Most mornings, Al the Cowman leaves the cafe by eight, heading directly west on the paved state highway to the dirt crossing over the Atchison, Topeka & Santa Fe tracks, then half a mile north on dirt and up the small promontory to the feedlot office. Al is what they call tough. He doesn't quit. He's tried wheat, beets, onions, pinto beans, corn, hogs, wheat again; and now, in a big way, it's cattle. Everything's riding on cattle, the whole damn family empire he began building thirty years ago with the little patch of wheat ground his uncle left him. But the markets have been bad for several years now, and Al is beginning to feel the strain. Stay, stick, and stall, he keeps telling himself, that's all a man can do. And privately wonders who in the family will rise to take his place in the coming half-century.

The two-way base station crackles incessantly in the dusty feedlot office. Al gets on the family channel and checks with his oldest son, Al Junior, to see if the corn's being watered up north. Then he calls his broker long-distance to get the futures. Perched precariously on a battered folding chair, he grunts into the telephone between man-sized chaws of Red Man, periodically spitting into a tin can, a coffee cup, an ashtray, whatever's handy. The futures are bad. He hangs up with a scowl on his face. Right now, Al is worried about old Banker Johnson, who he's sure has heard about those bad Arkie heifers that have been coming in. There's not much a man can do. Pay your money and take your chances. Bad shipments come along. But those last calves were pretty damn sorry; snot-nosed, eyes matted over, rib cages bulging out. Two were dead on the truck, five died during unloading. With a sigh Al takes down the adding machine and begins figuring up how many head he can afford to buy at the sale barn the next day with the proceeds from the fats to be trucked to slaughter later in the morning. But soon he tires and decides to head back into town again. Maybe face Banker Johnson. Maybe chew on the insurance man to get those death-loss payments from the last storm. Maybe just coffee at the liars' table. He grunts and mumbles to himself. "Time to call in the dog, lock the door, and piss on the fire." He mumbles to himself a lot these days.

For the first few weeks in June, the regulars at the liars' table don't quite know how to take me, nor I them. I learn their names by listening carefully to conversations I am excluded from, conversations conducted in a dialect so foreign to my ears that I literally fail to understand much of what I hear. It helps a great deal that Al the Cowman has opted to accept me. With a characteristically gruff mixture of respect and disdain, he takes to calling me the "mouthpiece," a moniker that sticks. I have just won Al an insurance settlement for several hundred head of fat cattle smothered by snow in a February storm; his stubborn Texas insurance company had originally balked at settling. I am hopeful that establishing a presence at the cafe will translate into more legal business, but during summer wheat harvest and on into fall corn and milo harvest business is slow. Nevertheless, to the discipline of hauling myself out of bed in darkness each morning to make the liars' table I add the discipline of opening my office by seven-thirty. Now and then men whose faces I have seen half concealed behind coffee cups at the cafe wait for me to get up from the table and follow me down Main Street to the office door. Without introducing themselves, their nervous fingers running over the creases in folded documents, they launch into halting explanations of little problems that have been bothering them for months, maybe years. Aunt Ellie's will, an insurance policy, the proposed gas royalty agreement tendered by some city slicker, a traffic ticket. I write letters for men involved in disputes over boundaries and well permits and cattle shipments, and I telephone district attorneys in three states to plead down traffic offenses. Banker Johnson up the street shuffles me some foreclosures and litigation, and I am still handling the irrigation farmers' suit against the natural gas company, but in my mind I'm wondering. Are they testing me? Will things pick up when the weather chills and the crops are in? Is this law office so obvious a front?

Agribusiness has pre-empted the state highway. Retail business lords it over Main Street.

Main Street. Properly speaking, a wide five-block tongue of hard-to-obtain asphalt extending right out of the gorge of the town, its northern tip licking into a dead-end intersection with the state highway. Stores cluster on two blocks of the street, the northernmost two blocks, the town's widest, smoothest ration of oiled blacktop. Almost all of the Main Street buildings are whitewashed

stucco or painted cement blocks; except for the Ace Theater, a free-standing metal round-top with a wood façade, and the old red-brick hotel, they are mortared tight up against their neighbors. It takes scarcely three minutes to walk down one side of Main Street and up the other, starting at City Market, then past the post office, Andy's Barber Shop, Jordan's Variety Store (the only place in town to buy a scrap of clothing), City Pharmacy, Town Foods, County National Bank, the Spa Hotel, Boston's Drugs, Dorsey's Auto Repair, AAA Hardware, Miller Pump and Casing; then across the wide boulevard at Oak Street to the Ace Theater and back north past Burton Electric, the Christian Book Store, the laundromat (a subsidiary of Boston's Drugs), Time-Out Luncheonette, an empty storefront (most recently the headquarters for a bankrupt building supply business, formerly a dry goods store), Pop's Barber Shop, Sally's Hair Boutique, Shorty's Cafe (closed and out of business), Herman's Real Estate and Insurance, Western Sprinkler Systems (formerly Garcia Chiropractic), and Arnold-Jackson Lumber. Farther south on Main Street is the First Baptist Church, next to it the new lawyer's office; hidden on side streets are the pool hall, two more hairdressers, an accountant, and the doctor's office. Outside the city limits are the Legion Club (five feet) and the liquor store (a mile) and, west on the state highway, the John Deere dealership, another fertilizer outlet, and the farm mercantile store run by Al the Cowman's youngest brother. The two feedlots are both north of town, Al's a mile west, his competitor's a mile east. The prevailing winds are southerly.

The largest town in the county is the county seat, twenty miles west; its population is two thousand compared to the town's nine hundred. There are no nonagricultural industries at all, anywhere in the county. No major trucking routes thread the county. There are no recreational amenities or governmental hubs enriching it, no trade schools or colleges or military installations. The terminal grain markets, packing houses, and shopping centers are three hundred miles away. There are, however, Sears and Wards catalogs, monthly visits from the Avon lady and the Rawleigh spice man, frequent make-up and Tupperware parties, occasional invasions of Texas oil and gas ventures that drill exploratory holes in farmers' wheat fields and mail service. And there are death and taxes and their spin-offs, two country lawyers in the county seat. There are two commercial banks, one in town and one in the county seat, but both are small and owned by the same out-of-state holding company with sense enough to know money turns over much faster in its midwestern urban hubs than it does in the county. And there is a savings and loan association seventy miles away. No more than half a day's drive distant there is available, within the constraints of red tape and the collateral value of land that misses three out of four wheat crops, agricultural borrowing at the Federal Land Bank, the Farmers Home Administration, and the Production Credit Administration.

But there is something about these few frayed and tenuous lifelines to the larger society that merely intensifies economic insularity. The higher-grade boot-cut Levis are not sold and worn on Main Street, but in Manhattan; and citizens of the county eat wilted lettuce and hamburgers ground from old cows while San Franciscans dine on the best cuts from choice steers and crisp greens. Transients gravitate to the town, because there is always work to do and not enough indigenous labor to do it. High-steppers hate the town, because shipping rates alone eliminate the margin for successful arbitrage. The big national agribusinesses carefully ration their machinery, chemical, fertilizer, and seed franchises in the county, because the secondary financing market carefully rations the supply of commercial paper in the county; and the Corn Belt, not the county, profits from the recent realization in banking circles that appreciating land values make agriculture a more attractive investment than it has ever been. The local economy, being so insular, violates every precept of economic rationalism. Yet, like the cowmen who stick and stall through the decades, a certain core merchant class survives and occasionally prospers.

Business picks up with the first frost, but I do not prosper as a lawyer. I could prosper, because even with my presence the legal services market in the county is still an oligopoly, and oligopoly is the linchpin of prosperity for purveyors of services and retail goods in the county. But I have a problem with billing. It is impossible for me to judge my scruffy-looking clients' ability to pay; time after time I learn too late that I have inappropriately discounted a bill because I have sized up a customer on the basis of his workday uniform, not his family name. Natives do not make this mistake. I am shocked at the fees I hear are charged by others for routine legal services. I am sometimes shocked at the quality of those services. As time goes by, I become aware of a decline in the quality of my own output. I am overworked, deprived of the rudimentary resources needed to do a good job. On big cases I am forced to drive hundreds of miles to avail myself of a decent law library. Given time, I fear, the freight charged on my product would become just as disproportionate to its quality as it is to the quality of the produce and baked goods at Town Foods, a prosperous local business.

During winter downtime, the farmers begin to come in. First come tentative inquiries about estate planning, stimulated by stories in farm journals about anticipated federal estate-tax reform; then some major land trades with tricky tax ramifications; then a bit of probate litigation and an actual jury trial. I incorporate a farm equipment dealership and several farming operations, negotiate cattle-feeding contracts and sales of agribusinesses. The real estate work overwhelms me, and hardly a day passes that I don't drive the twenty miles to the county seat to order a title abstract or check real property records. To avoid complicating our anthropological mission I make a rule not to handle divorce cases, then violate it in several hardship situations. To avoid displaying my incompetence I make a rule not to handle criminal matters, but violate it when, inevitably, the state circuit judge learns I'm around and favors me with court appointments to represent criminal indigents. I find myself frequenting the cell block in the new, LEAA-funded county jail and swapping stories with the sheriff and his deputies. A grain elevator, a propane dealer, and a seed company from out of state hire me to collect delinquent accounts. I try at least one traffic case a month and settle two for each one tried. I battle the IRS through three levels of administrative review to win a tax exemption for the research adjunct of the local state experiment station. The woman transcribing our interviews is forced to double as a legal secretary, and Jessica complains I am spending too little time on our project.

Yet the slapdash exercise in solo practice begins to bring benefits in community. It is as a lawyer, not as a writer of books, that I am initiated into the mysteries of Odd Fellowship, invited to attend city council meetings, and saluted at church or on Main Street. Jessica acquires an identity not as a teacher or sociologist, but as "the new lawyer's wife." And at the cafe, more and more farmers feel at home calling me the mouthpiece; they laugh, I laugh, and the moniker becomes a shortcut for relieving mutual awkwardness.

Half a block from the cafe, headed east, Al the Cowman surveys the pickups in the cafe parking lot: Peewee Jackson, the gas man, the town water man, the phone man. Al keeps driving, thinking without humor that a man'd be a damn sight smarter retiring or getting into one of them damn government deals than messing with cattle. At Main Street he turns south, his eyes reconnoitering the cars and pickups nosed in diagonally against the raised cement docks that support the cracking sidewalks. The vehicles help orient him as he makes up his mind where, and whether, to stop. The banker is out of the question for a spell, because three young farmers, none of whom has hit a good crop in recent years, are parked at County National; a haircut is out of the question, because the usual squad of pensioners, who remind Al of things he doesn't want to think about, has gathered at Andy's Barber Shop to discuss the wheat crop of 1922; picking up the mail is out, because the mail isn't up or Peewee Jackson wouldn't still be at the cafe; and grabbing a piece of beef jerky at City Market is out, because two of his cousins' old ladies are in from the country to buy out the store and visit everything in sight that talks.

Daunted, he continues south, pretending not to notice a wave from his cousin's fat old lady as he passes City Market, and heads out of town. Six miles south and two east he spends an hour fiddling with a center-pivot sprinkler he's just converted from gas to electricity. Then he heads back to town and steers the pickup into dock across the street from County National. He stays seated in the cab a few moments, assessing who is going to see him enter the bank. The mail's up now, but it's too early for the farmers to come in. Housewives and young mothers with baby strollers stand in unhurried groups on the Main Street sidewalks, trying before dinner to catch up on all the news their husbands got that morning at the cafe. The only males in sight are the Baptist preacher and the Jew who runs the picture show, both carrying mail and newspapers under their arms; the former smiling, waving, and strolling leisurely, the latter rushing along with his head down. No threat, Al concludes.

In the lobby of County National, two farmers are ahead of him. Al nods and slouches down in a chair near the wagon-wheel table Banker Johnson bought off of old Moon Jackson a year back. Al debates whether to get up and leave, not only because he's going to have to wait, but also because one of the waiting farmers, Will Schmidt, will probably start in with that Baptist deal any second. Not something a fella cares to discuss when he's got his mind on the bad Arkie heifers serving as collateral for the note he wants rewritten. But Al stays, and he is lucky. Will Schmidt is not in a proselytizing frame of mind. He's more concerned about covering his own cattle losses by fast-talking Banker Johnson into another twenty thousand dollars against the ten thousand dryland acres he bought up in 1936. "Just one or two good years," Will leans over and confides to Al, "that's all I need. Then maybe them boys'll take to callin' me 'Mr. Schmidt' again, not just 'ol' Will.'" Al chuckles.

At eleven-thirty, Banker Johnson comes out of the back office and beckons Al to enter; and the slow, delicate business begins, the lessons of thirty years of borrowing pitted against Banker Johnson's fear of the bank examiners.

Banker Johnson: A Different Breed of Cats

I guess I'd describe myself as a likeable person, a trustworthy person. I feel that I have, you know, a little knowledge and a little intelligence. I must, because I feel that if I didn't people wouldn't keep coming, asking me things just 'cause I'm their banker. I feel that I have compassion towards people, and I feel that people know that I do. They know that I love 'em and that I can work with 'em. And I think that the big majority like working with me. At least they've told me so. They've told me they don't want to bank someplace else, or didn't want to bank with anybody but me. You know, this gives you good feelings. It helps your ego anyway.

Frank Johnson is in his early fifties, a nervous man, a chain smoker. He is the one person who surely could leave. He has traveled extensively—Europe, Mexico, throughout the United States—and he loves fine art and contemporary popular novels. Like Abe Berkowitz, he has something of an outsider's eye, but he is a son of the Dust Bowl—he was born in Oklahoma twenty miles from where his grandfather homesteaded in the Oklahoma run—and in the Dust Bowl he stays.

The thing you get in a small country bank is the many joys, the many pleasures, besides all the agony and grief. If I would write a book as such about my banking life, I'd call it *The Agony and the Ecstasy.* The things I get to see, and the feelings I get to feel, are the joys of my farmers when they hit a crop or can pay off their notes. And the agony when they can't, when they miss a crop, or when the drought has hit them. Or the bugs have hit them. Or all the disasters have hit. There's many people that think all you have to do is plant a seed and it'll grow, and you harvest it, and you make a lot of money. Until you get out and do it, see the agonies, confront 'em, you have no idea.

In the forties, his father and his father's brothers built up a large national broomcorn brokerage from their Oklahoma home, and after World War II Frank became the company's manager in the county. He adopted the county seat as his home, for years living out of rented hotel rooms. When he saw the beginning of the domestic broomcorn market's collapse in the early sixties, he sold out his stock in the family concern and went into irrigation farming in the county. Four successive untimely frosts almost broke him. "If the good Lord was telling me not to farm, I apologize for all the other farmers that froze out too, because we weren't the only ones. But I did quit farming at that time, and I went into the fertilizer business." Then the banker in town offered him a job; he saw a chance to get himself out of debt. "I started as assistant cashier, worked as a loan officer. Later came cashier and vice-president, executive vice-president. Then president." An out-of-state holding company bought out the local owner of the bank, but Frank stayed on. He has a difficult job: tight credit, leery correspondents, tumbling commodity prices, absentee higher-ups.

This past year, we had some disastrous hails. I don't ever recall seeing an irrigated pasture completely wiped out by hail, so that there wasn't even a stub left. Alfalfa was the same way. It was just snubbed off there, and with rain behind the hail it just washed out the fields. One day there was a foot of alfalfa, and the next day there was nothing there. Just bare ground. I don't know. The ones that get hurt, your heart just bleeds for 'em. Or it does for me.

Even though you're the banker, you know all these people personally too. You know their families, you know their kids, their in-laws. You're not working with a number, with just another loan customer. You're working with somebody that you know, almost to the point where you're personally involved . . . even though you're not actually. You get personally involved, I think, if you have love in your heart. You love these people. I would call that personally involved. We have seen so many disasters and various types of catastrophes: droughts and heat and hot winds and bugs and hail, strong winds and snowstorms. You just have to bleed for them, love 'em.

Of course, the thing about being president of a bank is that you do have a lot of power. You have a lot of power over the people, and you have a lot of power over their lives, because the way you disburse them money governs their life. Maybe a wrong decision could turn their life patterns completely around. When you get into farm operations, diversified farm operations, you really do govern their lives. It's not like just buying an automobile or something.

Most of my customers come in and ask me for advice. Commodities, cattle, stocks, bonds, insurance. I guess in an area where there's not very many professional people, you're just about everything to them. People come in, you know, "Would you read my Medicare insurance and see if it's good?" Or other people come in, "Would you read this insurance policy and see if it's what I want?" Well, I don't know what they want. "Well, you know my financial position, and do I need this? Can I afford this?" You have people come in and say, "Frank, I'm sick, I need an operation. Can I afford it?" (He chuckles.) You have people coming in and say, "I'm in real bad mental condition. I'm about to go crazy. Do you think I should go see a psychiatrist? Could I afford a psychiatrist?" I guess I'm saying that you get to be jack-of-all-trades. Not only in your farming end but in all strains of life. You're it. You're supposed to know everything. You're the banker, you're there for advice. I feel that they're coming in and asking me for a little bit of my knowledge. To me, it's a very important job. If you really feel that you want to help your farmers, your local people, to the best of your abilities, it's an awesome responsibility. If you take it to heart.

Shortly before we arrive in the county, a minor scandal occurs. An Arkansas evangelist turned entrepreneur gets into the bank's pockets for tens of thousands of dollars of construction loans, then goes belly-up and skips. The loans were processed by a junior loan officer (also from Arkansas) whom Frank had hired, and neither the examiners nor the higher-ups nor the local citizenry are convinced the Arkansas connection is a mere coincidence. I am retained to help clean up the resultant mess of foreclosures, bankruptcy claims, and lawsuits.

Frank and I talk business frequently, informally; and without ado I ease unofficially into a house-counsel role. There is something more than business that draws together the graying, impeccably attired country banker and the young city lawyer who has slowly adjusted to Levi's and cowboy boots. I take to dropping by his office at the bank almost daily after retrieving the mail. We drink coffee and talk about art, farming, prices, ideas for books—his favorite is a Harold Robbins-type epic to be titled Harvest*—and schemes for making money.*

I think as you grow older, you get more satisfied with life, you get more accustomed to it. You look back on your life, and you look at things you did to people that you wish you could undo. Things that you said, things you did, things that you didn't do, things you should've done. In the earlier parts of my life I didn't have the concern towards other people. In your younger days, you're a little more cocky, you're a little more feisty, you're wanting to get someplace a little faster.

Now, I think I can appreciate the time element of a work of art. I can understand a beautiful painting that a man sits down and paints in a day, a week, but to sit there and work on a statue for five years or something—it's just unbelievable! The most fascinating to me is the *Pietà*, the workmanship, the detail he put into it. The fine lines, for instance, on the clothing. He's got—what?—a sixteenth of an inch of marble? I guess Michelangelo's my favorite. Once we were in a Bible study, and a person, they said to me, "What do you think God looks like?" And I said, "Well, he's gray-haired, and he has this long white beard, and he has a pretty good-sized nose, but you can tell he has a big chin, and he's pointing to a man, reaching out." Anyway, everybody was giving their version of what they thought God looked like, and that was mine.

What keeps you here?

I don't know why I stay in this country. I guess I've seen some of the most beautiful spots of the world; the wind doesn't blow, and you get ample rainfall. You know, there isn't anything more depressing to me than wind blowing. There isn't anything more depressing. And if the dirt is blowing with it, then it's even more depressing. I get real depressed even in these dust-blowing days we still have today periodically. When you see a dirt storm coming, it affects you. You remember things. You think that maybe someday you might go to one of those beautiful spots and retire there. That might be your paradise. But when you really get to thinking, you wouldn't want to leave your friends, leave all the things you have here in this great country.

Your roots are here. The most beautiful people in the world live here. It's hard to describe them. It's a feeling you have. There are people that have left this country, and they're gone for two or three years or something. They think paradise is somewhere else, but pretty soon they're back. Every time I go away, I miss this county. I can hardly wait to get home. It's real hard to describe. I can't say that it's just the wide open spaces, because there's wide open spaces other places in the world, in the United States. You can't say that it's all people, because there's good people in every place. But they are a different breed of people here. I feel it, and I know it, but I can't say that I can describe it. Whether it's the hard knocks they take, or that they live together, or what. . . .

I have heard people say that, well, people in this community are so close. And they are to a certain extent, but if you try to organize 'em they're the most disorganized band of people in the world. You can't talk to 'em, you can't get two of 'em to think alike. You see, they're together, they're joined together by something, but at the same time they're . . . well, they're the most disorganized organized people that I've seen. (He chuckles.) They're independent, basically. Each one is very proud, they're proud in their own right. If an outsider comes in and says something bad, anything bad about this county, or anything about this area, they're in trouble. It doesn't make any difference where they're from, you're gonna have yourself trouble if you talk bad about this county. I don't know what it is. All I know is that I can feel it. I'm thinking of grit. They do have grit with their pride. They survive hard times, and they're proud they've survived, they're proud they didn't leave in the thirties and in the forties and fifties. They didn't quit during the droughts, and they went through the dust storms, and they feel they can still survive 'em if they come again.

One year we have a little more rain than another, but basically it's droughty all the time. There's never a time that we have really ample rainfall. We'll always basically have a drought. But we live with this. We know if it's raining this week, it's going to be dry next week. But we're going to survive it, and I think that's your pride. I feel it. I feel it myself. I think we have pride of our businessmen as much as we do with our farmers. We all rely on our farmers, so we're part of farming, even though we don't go out and farm. We have pride with ourselves, because we survive these rough times too. We're proud of our farmers, and we're proud of ourselves. In this country, it's just . . . it's different. We're a different breed of cats, I guess.

3 Men at Work

Somebody who knows how to back a cattle truck.

A county brand inspector's definition of a cowboy

I remember a magazine, I can't remember the name. Anyhow, they interviewed a family out in Arizona complaining about the high price they had to pay for food. They didn't know how they was going to pay for their boat and the swimming pool and two television sets and two cars and all that. Well, maybe they ought to bring their ass out here and see how it's produced and they wouldn't complain so much.

A cow boss at Al the Cowman's feedlot

THE FIELDS

The August sun is relentless. It bleaches the fields and fades the brightly hued seed-company caps worn by the farmers to the fields, the cafe, the bank, the bathroom. Beneath the jutting hat brims, human skin is baked a weathered bronze to just above the eyebrows; and from March, when the winds begin, till after fall harvest, when they relent, over the bronze is the ubiquitous film of grit. It is tasted, it is smelled, it cannot be escaped.

The days melt into one another. The fields are now a patchwork of mature cornstalks, rows of russet maize, ravaged expanses of last year's wheat stubble ground up into vast planes of raw, clodded dirt waiting to be sown. Day after day since spring, farmers and hired men and wetbacks have clambered on the green, red, and silver tractors dragging Rube Goldberg attachments, alternately leveling, weeding, chiseling, and smoothing the prospective wheat fields. Twelve, fourteen, sixteen hours a day, following the sun and the high-beamed tractor headlights, they lumber forward at two, three, four miles per hour, tracing the rectangular perimeter of sections, half sections, quarters. One mile east, a half mile north, one mile west, a half mile south. Repeat. Like Russian dolls that fit into one another, the tours get smaller and smaller. And the rhythm is interrupted only for the noontime break: cold beans and Vienna sausage or sardines from cans, or spiced beans wrapped in a soft-shelled tortilla, or, for the ones with big crews and contempt for nature's deadlines, a hot chicken fry and mashed potatoes and white bread at the cafe. A dozen times a day, the flawless sky is scrutinized for the telltale gray that so often deceives but sometimes rewards. A dozen times a day the need for moisture is discussed. "If we could only get a little moisture." As if the saying would make it so.

One night there is thunder and lightning and rain. The rain beats fiercely against windows, and farmers sleep and awaken many times in the dark to listen to the lullaby so long in coming. The morning rising is leisurely. Too much coffee is consumed at the cafe; no one will go to the fields today. Rain gauges are checked, and phone calls crisscross the county.

"What'd you get?"

"We got two and thirty-hundredths."

"Over north, they got three."

The rain continues through the morning. Mud is tracked on rugs, but even the most finicky housewives do not complain. On Main Street, merchants smile broadly and almost seem to gloat at each new entry in their charge-account files. Television slips into the quiet, misty afternoon. The county exhales a collective sigh of relief. Nature has cooperated. There will be enough moisture to sow the wheat. The cycle can continue. Whatever the outcome.

Again: days melt into one another. The dark, rain-soaked earth is bleached dusty brown. The hot winds blow. The earth's surface hardens and cakes and cracks. Again: Snub-nosed tractors, looking ever so much like children's electric train engines, dot the fields, kicking up clouds of dust and exhaling black plumes of exhaust from tall smokestacks as they traverse the squares of wheat

ground; one after another they cut the soil deeply and turn it, locking the invisible jewels of moisture in the earth's secret pockets.

Will it rain again before mid-September? Should the winter wheat be drilled a full five inches deep? Will the green bugs be bad again this year? Did old man Fainey *really* start to drill already? The unanswerable questions must be reviewed. And each farmer must climb in his pickup, drive along the rutted field roads to the fields, get out, dig into the ground, and agonize over the odds. Inexorably, decisions get made. The hired men and the wetbacks are told to load the drills on flatbed trailers and haul out the bags of seed.

It takes half a day to attach the drills to the tractor. Four drills per tractor, each an awkward octopede with a seed bin and eight sharp-toed feet to rip the soil and deposit the seed. Thirty-two spear feet in all, spaced twelve inches apart. Eighteen pounds of seed per acre of ground. And, behind each of the thirty-two shanks, a press wheel to follow and pack new dirt over the pellets. All morning there is the clang of hammers, the dull grinding of wrenches, the whir of expanding rulers. At last the drills are properly spaced and secured, and the pink blight- and bug-treated seeds are poured from fifty-pound bags into the seed bins.

Marking the field and making the initial planting tour is ritually reserved for the farmer himself. Moving cautiously along the border of the field, he glances frequently out the rear cab window and then back to the undisturbed dirt vista in front of him. Debris along the edge of the field causes delays. He stops often to get out and lug away obstructions: rocks from the walls of old homesteads, rusty fragments of bedsprings, an old well casing. More forward progress and more stops. Tufts of Russian thistle wrap around the drill's spearpoints. The farmer gets out to remove them and feels a welcome chill back inside the air-conditioned cab. The thistles are removed but not carted away; they will keep the ground from blowing and protect the seed in coming months.

So it proceeds. Forward progress and frequent pauses. At the end of the field, the corner is turned. The tractor groans against its own wheels. Two more turns and back to the beginning point. The small marker wheel, flung out to the side of the tractor on a hydraulic arm, has established the course for the next round. Soon the hired man can take over. It will take him twenty-two moving hours to plant a half section. It will take another five or six hours to stop and refill the seed bins and clear away the thistles and obstructions. If all goes well, the seed will germinate in two days. In five days, the infant plant will break through the earth's crust. In three months, a green bristle will appear on the earth's surface. In five months, the bristle will challenge the suffocating onslaught of dry, blowing snow. In seven months, heartbreakingly vast patches of the greenness will be gone, and the ground plowed and turned for another round of gambling: maize will be spring-planted, and the banker will have to wait. Other patches will grow into tall and sturdy green wheat plants, and after nine months they will have sprouted heads and ripened and dried to golden hue. And in ten months, once again seed, the wheat will fill semis and elevators and corrugated-metal storage bins. If all goes well.

Mike Klimm: Going Forward

He is the first of only two persons to make overtures to us before we can make overtures to him. In our second month in the county, we decide to attend a public banquet sponsored by the National Farmers' Union in the next county north. Tony Dechant, the national president, gives a speech, and the Kitchen Klatter Band—housewives with wooden spoons and pots and washboards—provides entertainment. The fare is ribs and overdone pot roast. The farmers in attendance are scrubbed, leisure-suited, and hatless, white foreheads set off by sunburned noses and cheeks. After the banquet, Mike Klimm strides up and introduces himself. He is in his late twenties, tall, of medium build. He is wearing fancy dress boots, two-tone tan and white. He has heard we've moved down and why ("I figured you had to be the ones; I recognize everybody else"), and he volunteers a brief account of himself. Graduate degree in physics, just back farming in the county the last several years, living by himself in a trailer out in the country. There is no time to exchange telephone numbers, and we don't even catch his last name. Several weeks later we make inquiries in town and telephone to invite him for supper at our house. When he arrives, we lamely explain we've also got a tape-recorded interview in mind. He smiles. "I kind of suspected as much when I agreed to come."

I'm neither fish nor fowl. A substantial part of me is urban, fairly well-developed appreciation of urban values, and a substantial part of me—so much of me—is rural. So I say I'm neither fish nor fowl. I don't completely fit either place. Rather indeterminate. (He pauses and furrows his brow.) It's really hard, really hard at times. It's difficult sometimes, along the lines of what do you speak of, who do you visit with? That's part of the problem. There's different values that are shared. You're not going to find anyone to exchange values with in this country. Anyway, I haven't.

The first evening of food and tape recorders is followed by others. Mike is primed for the interviews, and even when we eventually stop running the machine he talks with the care of one who expects to be quoted. It is a joy for us to meet someone so articulate on the subject of farming and county mores, but we learn far more about Mike Klimm from what he doesn't say and what others tell us than from what he is willing to impart. He explains how a love for books and an interest in solid state physics propelled him to the state agricultural college and later to grad school at the University of Illinois. "I didn't start driving a tractor until I was maybe eleven years old. You can't really handle a tractor too well before about that age. But reading was what I did in my spare time. And I led, I suppose, a rather normal existence, apart from the fact that I had an appreciation for books and ideas, thoughts."

He is lonely, and he works long hours. He and his brother raise dryland wheat and cattle. He takes an interest in state Democratic politics, the policies of the local agricultural stabilization board, new developments in farm technology. He wants badly to find a niche for himself in the county, but the farmers a generation older remember his long hair and heretical views back in 1970, when the invasion of Cambodia finally revolted him so much he decided to come back home rather than pursue the education that might have led him to work in a lab at Motorola or RCA. Now his hair is short, almost crewcut. Since we left the county, he has sometimes made the long drive to the city to visit us. He seems moody, depressed, less and less certain he'll stay. Then, in the fall of 1977, the county revolts and Mike finds a niche. He is seen on television, quoted in the newspapers, and summoned to the microphone to expatiate on the demands of the American Agriculture Movement.

I never did have problems adjusting to being in the city when I went away to school. I didn't have particularly a young-man-from-the-provinces complex. You know, the only way I can make something of my life is to get away from where I come from. That idea was brought up by Clifton Fadiman and several others. My younger brother and I had been doing all the farming since I was seventeen, and the year I graduated from high school Father became ill and died three years later. So I could have returned to the farm any time. But there was still something out there that was keeping me away. From day one when I learned to read, there were other worlds out there. I was sort of like Lionel Trilling's *Of This Time, Of That Place.* I really believed, much like Trilling's protagonist, that there was the world of ideas, and there is the relation to the cosmos. (He laughs.) I'm fascinated by that sort of activity.

But you came back.

Yeah. (He pauses.) I got the realization in college, in grad school, that farming—the value system of farming—was much more a part of my make-up than I had initially believed. I need more positive and tangible reinforcement, you know, apart from the rewards of purely cerebral activity. It's not quite the dirty hands that I enjoy so much, as such. It's not quite so complex and philosophical an issue or anything. I didn't immediately read Sartre and decide to return to the farm. (He laughs.)

Each year, I raise a crop. I have a feel for the grain, harvest it or not harvest it as the case may be, and I raise a calf crop each year. That sort of thing. And being outdoors, being able to work outdoors—not vacationing, but living outdoors. A substantial part of the time, I found that just meant an awful lot to me, and simply on the basis of capital and experience I had the opportunity to go into something like farming. Which to a jillion and one people I know in the city is the romantic ideal. It was within my means and ability, and it fit me. Rather well. And I imagine I'll always be involved in agriculture—not necessarily here, there's nothing particularly magic about this county. I do have family ties here, but I think my ties are more with the soil than they are with anybody in particular.

What are ties to the soil? What does that mean?

To me, it means ties to the basics, that sense you get, that good feeling within yourself from being able to provide for your basic needs. A more fundamental existence, not so highly artificial. You provide for what you need. If you want to take the time to raise a garden, you can have everything, although if you raise commercial wheat or cattle like I do, you may be restricted. But still, you're raising something to provide your basic needs. With a couple of sheep, you could have wool and you could make your own garments. That sort of thing isn't done in commercial farming communities, but it's still that basic leaning in your activity. And I think—well, Margaret Mead observed it in *Male and Female*—perhaps it's the driving thing that ties men in particular to the soil as opposed to women. It's the concept of the male going forward, and he sees it, through his progeny, through his sons. You know, farming is a skill; it's handed down, largely from father to son. So you're tied to the soil by providing for your family, also as an extension of yourself.

I know I feel that, and I know my father felt that and was damn dismayed that I didn't want to pursue farming. I mean, my God, what's the matter with you? I was a bit young, I suppose, and didn't have the basic understanding that this was what Dad had worked for, all his life, really. Busted his ass so that one or both of us kids could continue the farming, and then neither one of us showed too much interest in it. My brother a bit more than I, but, hell, I was going to study physics and be an industrial physicist. (He laughs.)

There's layer after layer of tradition here. There's a lot of continuity. I know certainty in myself, what I've seen happen to me; my values have become more traditional . . . emphasis on family as an ideal, as a central role, a part of me in the community and in my life. The change has sort of been by osmosis. I read much the same things I did while I was in college, but I've come to believe some structure must be established to carry on the basic functions of civilization from one generation to the next. I don't think swinging singles activity for a lifetime is going to promote anything that will last. I feel a deep responsibility for the next generation. I don't know, once you get away from the weekend-oriented society, the hedonistic approach that characterizes the city, you see that it won't work in a rural community. Hell, there's too damn much work to do. Perhaps it's a bit of maturing on my part as far as wanting to take more responsibility for generations to come, that I'm becoming more traditional, more conservative. Once the responsibility is yours, it becomes a bit harder to be Daedalus.

After the Klimm calves have been worked in the fall, Mike invites us to enjoy the dividend, a mountain oyster fry at his brother's home in the county seat. There are four young couples present, and while the women fry up calf nuts in the kitchen the men sit in front of the color television console in the living room, drinking bourbon and Cokes and talking farming and hunting. The men are Mike's age or younger, but their children are already shooting rabbits with .22s and riding motorbikes. The men talk around Mike, almost as if he weren't in the room. When he complicates a discussion of wheat prices by mentioning foreign grain sales, he is rudely interrupted.

Who do I talk to down here? My dog. (He laughs.) Men here are just inarticulate. It's part of a pattern, an ideal, that maybe evolved from—well, okay, what do you do with your leisure time? Do you read? Do you cultivate arts, letters? The answer is no. The prototype for a hero is a stereotype, and it's John Wayne, the John Wayne mentality. You don't have to be particularly articulate, but you should be forceful. Not only "Duh." But "DUH!" And it's sort of hard. It's sort of a shame, because there's a wealth of knowledge to be had in rural life, but yet it isn't developed and formalized by rural people. There aren't that many people here raising different crops that even know that much about botany. They have sort of a working field knowledge, and in a sense, hell, they don't have to know what the hell makes a plant grow. A plant knows what to make a plant grow. Why do we have to know? You know, we get up and harvest the grain.

It's a question of *homo ludens* versus *homo faber*. That's the dominant theme of our life. Here, it's *homo faber*. Essentially, we define ourselves by our work. You ask somebody how they are. They start off by saying, "Well, we got some rain over here last week, and we're back over here getting ready to move cattle, fifteen miles north." Or something like that. Okay, you ask someone in the city, "How are you?" A discourse on the flaws in his life and the heavens and whether he and his wife have done anything meaningful in terms of new sexual roles. No telling what answer you get there. Here, we're just sort of plodding along. "Well, you know, could be better." (He laughs.) People don't talk about themselves. They are what they are in terms of how they make their living . . . rather than, you know, their relation to the cosmos. But I pretty much talk like everybody else down here in general conversations. I cuss with the best of them, and I get along with some of the most rustic characters you ever saw in your life. Guys that say, you know, "Hitched my car up and went into the store." And you know they mean every word of it. They hitched their car up and walked into the store. Talk with the weirdest expressions you ever heard in your life. That's the way they are. That's the way they talk. (He laughs.)

What do you think about when you drive the tractor?

Girls I've known. (He laughs.) Girls I'd like to know. (He laughs again.) Business. Sometimes I listen to the radio, but most of the time I don't. I've always got something going—people I know or something. I think I've got a hyperactive mind. Nothing's really boring to me, so one activity fades out, I can always think of something, and I suppose I'm sort of fortunate in that respect. I enjoy farming and ranching. I'm not ever really bored. Tired, ticked off, you know, standing out in a 105-degree sun or a thirty-mile-an-hour wind, trying to fix fence or get some damn crazy cow back in.

One thing I do miss is that sort of lively discussion and encounter with someone who's got a nodding acquaintance with some of the things that I appreciate. There are a couple of people in the county seat, but, you know, I'm sort of a loner and busy; and I don't get out and mix much with the new schoolteachers in town or that sort of thing. But that's pretty much it. It's just sort of a lonely life for a kindred spirit. (He pauses.) But it's not all that bad. If loneliness or being alone is for the most part solitude rather than loneliness, it's just not all that bad. But, hell, I might end up being a bachelor for the rest of my life with an attitude like that. I do miss a certain type of companionship. (He pauses.) Rather fiercely miss it, I suppose. But I knew what I was giving up when I left the city.

THE SMELL OF MONEY

July and August are hot and dry, as usual. Grass is scarce, as usual, and alfalfa hay is priced out of reach. The market is sluggish, as usual, and at the livestock commission companies, better known as sale barns, the weekly sales start late and finish early. Proud Sam Wilson, a solo rancher who makes his living calling auctions when he's not raising commercial cattle and building a herd of registered Brangus, starts out from home at six-thirty in the morning Mondays and Wednesdays. Home is his deceased father's ranch, now remodeled, down on a bend in Big Horse Creek, a mile west of Sam's Aunt Minnie Sue (ninety years old and the first white woman born in the county) and half a mile north of Sam's brother Jim Joe, also a solo rancher. The sale barn where Sam calls Monday sales is 130 miles to the northwest over winding, deserted dirt ranch roads. The barn where he calls Wednesday sales isn't quite so far away.

A hot July day. I arrive at the Wilson ranch wearing new jeans, new boots, and a new straw hat, feeling every bit as uncomfortable as the day before, when I met him for the first time: "So you're writing a book about ranchers and farmers," he drawled. "Well, seems to me anybody writin' that kinda book oughta come out and see how it's done." He waves me down to a holding pen in the corrals behind the barn, where he and his boys have gathered seventy-five baby calves, each a mere three to four hundred pounds. The men rode out horseback early that morning and cut the calves from their mothers in the pasture, and now the mothers fidget and moo hysterically for their babies outside the corral fence. An electric branding iron in one hand, Sam stands and tells me what they're doing as one of his boys wades into the huddled calves, grabs one violently by a hind leg, and jerks it out of the herd onto the clear ground. His other boy moves in and grabs the calf by the opposite foreleg, and together they throw the animal to the ground, the one sitting across its neck and bending back the foreleg, the other bracing a boot in the calf's butt and pulling away and back on the hind leg. A cigarette dangling from the corner of his mouth, Sam moves in with the electric iron, waits for the calf to stop twitching, and applies the hot coils to the left rear flank. As the calf wriggles and squirms and bleats, billows of yellowish-white smoke envelope Sam. He holds his breath against the stench of burning hair and hide, squints, lifts the iron, lets the smoke clear, then reapplies it. When he lifts the iron a second time, there is a clear brand on the pink, scorched hide. "It's a bull," one of the sons declares. Sam looks at me and grins. "Now we got 'im down, we're gonna cut his nuts off." He takes a pocketknife from his pocket, opens the blade, and reaches for the exposed scrotum. The calf squirms, but the boys secure their respective holds. Sam jabs the point of the knife through the middle of the bag and with a grunt yanks upwards, making a clean cut. With both hands, he squeezes a testicle out from the blood-wet, pink interior; it's white and blue-veined, about the size of a small plum. Sam grabs it with his right hand and begins to pull, slowly but firmly. The testicle cord comes out: six inches, a foot, a foot and a half. Pulling with his right hand, he uses his left to peel back the tissue and mucous coating of the cord in sure, swift strokes. When the cord is as thin as kite string, he reaches back inside with the knife and cuts the cord as deep into the bag as he can. The process is repeated for the other testicle, and then Sam sprays the scrotum area with aerosol disinfectant. As he works, he explains that he castrates the way his father taught: slitting the bag "against the grain" and reaching inside for the nuts, not just cutting the bottom off the bag and letting the nuts pop out the way they do at the feedlots; his method, he says, abets healing.

The bull calf, now a steer calf, has little two-inch horns, which Sam removes with a device like an apple corer, digging deep into the animal's forehead around the horns' circumfer-

ence. The calf bleats, its thick tongue pushes out of its mouth, and geysers of blood squirt up into the air, covering Sam's face, arms, and shirt. He applies blood-stopping powder to the wounds and hands me a syringe. "Five cc's under the hide, right here in the neck." I shoot in the antibiotic, my hands trembling uncontrollably. That done, Sam and I stand back, and his boys release their grips and jump away. The calf leaps to its feet and bounds back to the herd, letting out a final bleat of terror.

By the time I've assisted on ten more "workings," the process begins to seem less terrifying. I wade into the herd and drag out a few myself, helping to throw them to the ground and restrain them. The smells are good, the sky is clear, the work is hard, and the physical struggles with the animals are exhilarating. I begin to notice the skill more than the gore of the cutting (which changes the bull's mind from "ass to grass") and of the dehorning (which eliminates the risk of infection from goring and makes the herd look more uniform for market). I am fascinated by the strength, anatomy, and stupidity of the cattle. When all seventy-five calves have been worked, Mrs. Wilson serves up a ten-dish hot dinner in the air-conditioned ranch house. I do not appreciate it yet, but in scrapping around in the dirt with these dumb critters under the big sky I have tasted something of the illusion: just cows and calves and your own place and being free.

Until several years ago, Sam also called sales on Fridays at a barn two hundred miles over the state line. He'd leave at five in the morning and get back home at three or four the next morning. Although Sam's way of life is very important to him, he cut out the Friday auctions when the doctor told him it might cease to be a life. But that's just the kind of deal that makes Sam shake his head in disgust every so often as he chain-smokes and drives along with his foot to the floor in Old Blue, his rusty pickup, on his way to the sales. You've got to have something else to keep you going. Cattle, the way it works out, ends up a hobby.

Sam breathes a little easier when, heading west, farm country is completely behind him. It isn't exactly a generational grudge, because Sam is too young to remember the pivotal invasions of sod busters. But he has an almost primordial sense that God intended the county for cattle. The sod busters broke it up, brought the dust, drained off the good artesian well water, and then, in Sam's own lifetime, drew down the water table so low a man can't water stock without a thousand-foot well. The ranch country panorama has a soothing effect on Sam. The scruffy buffalo grass is somehow clinging to the parched earth's crust, and last spring's calf crop looks sleeker and fatter than it has any right to. Still, when he winds around a big bend in the road and finds himself looking out on the Masterton spread, his frustration bubbles over again. Those damn federal grazing permits. Guys like Bill Masterton who've got a lock on them can ranch all their lives without having to worry about a mortgage payment to the bank. It's not fair. How can a guy compete if he's having to buy his own land as well as run stock on it? "They're driving the little guy out," Sam mutters to himself. "But there's gonna be a payday."

A "starvation trap," Bill Masterton jokingly calls his thousands of acres of permitted Forest Service grazing land. Bill is sixty, looks seventy. He is arthritic, about five-ten, in possession of a gargantuan pot belly, fleshy faced and heavy lipped. He has short sandy hair and wears his blue jeans slung lower than can be believed without being seen.

We take off through the pastures in his pickup, driving from "brood to brood" (Bill's words). A few bulls are lounging about the pastures, but the summer breeding season is drawing to a close. (Mrs. Masterton says: "See that old bull over there just lazyin' around? He's about through with his job. Unless some cow said she had a headache, he'd make her wait.") The Masterton calves will come in January and February, when the herd is in the lowland winter pastures. There will follow a spring roundup, when the new calves are worked and branded, and then the whole herd of cows and calves will be run on the summer uplands. In the fall the calves will be rounded up again and weaned; the majority of young steers and heifers will be cut off for market. Bill has buyers who come to the ranch from hundreds of miles to buy up his annual crop. The best heifers are "topped" (kept for breeding purposes), and some of the old cows get culled and sent to the feedlot. Meanwhile, the breeding cows and heifers have been bred again in July and August, and a new crop is on its way. At calving time, Bill and his wife bring the heifers up to the corral by the house and check them hourly. First calves are almost always difficult. Sometimes you use a winch and chain to drag the newborn calf forcibly from its mother's womb.

The Mastertons' Hereford cows and calves are sleek and handsome. Their coats are fluffy and glint in the sun. Their rib cages do not show. Bill, however, refuses to laud the crop. He says the cattle speak for themselves. We go back to the house for T-bones from a Masterton steer. Bill reduces his T-bone to its essence, using a sharp knife and his teeth. Mrs. Masterton says he gets 'em so clean she can't even give 'em to the dogs.

Wherever cattle and cowmen gather, a fecal, acrid odor hangs in the air. Call it the smell of excitement, of dreams, even of life itself. In the county, they call it the smell of money. It tickles Sam Wilson's nose even before he steps out of his pickup in the sale barn's parking lot. He revives.

But with prices down and rain scarce, almost everyone is hurting. Only a few commissionable agents for packing houses, which are not hurting, and a diehard band of cowmen, who mostly don't know what else to do, show up for the summer sales. Inside the high-ceilinged sale barn, these bandy-legged holdovers from the nineteenth century with tanned faces and straw cowboy hats and big barrel chests gather in groups of four or five to pass the time until the sale begins. They chat about the bleakness of the money market and futures, about the rumors of brucellosis outbreaks and back-tagging crackdowns by the feds. "By God, I tell ya, these damn sonovabitches in this money deal make the whole shittin' thing go 'round. I ain't shittin' you, by God, them ole boys can do it now." Sam nods. Somebody says a good word about his son's bull-riding performance in a local rodeo. Sam smiles. A few of the men begin kidding each other about rodeo misadventures of their own youth. Somehow, though, there is a little too much effort in the bantering; too many sets of broad fleshy shoulders seem to slump.

Just before noon, a sale barn hand wets down the sand in the ring with a garden hose. In winter, the sale would run from ten till ten, and it would take Sam and another auctioneer twelve hours of alternating two-hour shifts to sell off all the stock. Today, Sam will manage the whole thing in six hours with just a few breaks to rest his voice. At twelve sharp, he clambers up behind the auction block. A ring man and the sale barn owner slip into the ring. The owner yanks open a gate, and in stumbles a haggard old cow, alone and confused. She looks from side to side, frog-eyes the ring man, shies, runs back to the closed gate, whirls, plants her feet, snorts. The ring man cracks a whip. The cow balks, whirls again, runs for a corner, feinting at the ring man with a jagged, menacing horn. He jumps for safety to the second fence rail. The sale barn owner shouts out the starting bid.

"Twenty-five DOLLAR!"

"HUP!" cries the first ring man.

"HUP-HUP!" cries the second ring man.

And Sam Wilson begins his chant.

"ALL RIGHT! Goin' by the pound. TWENTY-FIVE! Twenty-five-dollar-bid-it-bid-it-bid-it-to-buy-quarter-now-half-a-dollar-now-seventy-five-who'll-give-six-an'-a-quarter-for-'er? Six-an'-a-quarter-half-a-dollar-seventy-five-seven-dollar!"

"HUP!" cries a ring man.

"WE GOT twenty-seven-now-a-quarter-seven-dollar-bid-it-to-buy-'er-quarter-half-a-dollar-bid-it-to-buy-'er-seventy-five-seventy-five-seventy-five-bid-it-to—"

"HUP!" cries a ring man.

"EIGHT DOLLAR! Bid-it-to-buy-'er-twenty-eight-an'-a-quarter-eight-an'-a-quarter—EIGHT AN' A DIME! Twenty-eight-dollar-bid-now-ten-gimme-ten-ten-bid-it-to-bid-it-bid-it-bid-it-to buy-'er-ten-gimme-ten-for-'er-bid-it-bid-it-bid-it-to-buy-'er-twenty-eight-dollar-bid-now-ten-bid-now-ten-I'm-a-gonna-get-ten-gonna-get-ten-for-'er—I SOLD 'ER! TWENTY-EIGHT DOLLAR: TO Number Forty-one."

Sold, the cow is shooed from the ring to be weighed and ticketed to the buyer whose assigned auction number is forty-one. Sam takes a drag on his cigarette and a quick sip of water. The owner opens the gate again. Four cows with unweaned calves stumble into the ring. The cows are sold by the pound, the calves for a flat price. Sam, who knows all the buyers by their assigned numbers, relies on the ring men to flag bids. The buyers communicate bids through anything as blatant as a flick of the index finger, as subtle as a raised eyebrow. A cowman in a buying frame of mind does not like to flaunt it, especially in these depressed summer sales.

Cattle in, cattle out, the sale grinds surely forward. The order buyers for the packing houses fill their orders of old cows and bargain steers, the speculators buy up the mangiest calves in hopes of a quick resale a hundred miles away at a small markup, and the slump-shouldered regulars chew, spit, and wonder whether to bring their spring crop in the following week or to take a gamble on a rain, some grass growth, a better price come fall.

Occasionally the summer winds shift and blow into town from the northeast or northwest, bringing with them the smell of money that swirls and eddies about the two feedlots north of town. The smell seeps through doorways and into air-conditioning systems and permeates clothing like a foul gas. The town folk wrinkle their noses and make sour faces, but they also wink and make jokes, because the smell of money from the feedlots signifies jobs for otherwise unemployable young men with families and fair prices for huge quantities of local grain.

Not unlike the sulfurous fog overhanging a great steel city, the feedlot smell of money of the last decade signals the sacrifice of individual effort to collective enterprise, the marshaling of capital and labor to rational, profit-making objectives. Each year, thousands and thousands of animals arrive at the feedlots, forty or fifty head per cattle truck, to be initiated into the age of gluttony. They come as three- and four-hundred-pound calves from Florida, Alabama, and Arkansas, gaunt and ornery Angus and Brahmans who have never seen human beings. They come as six-, seven-, and eight-hundred-pound feeder steers and heifers from the ranches of local cowmen. They come as sick and sterile and infirm cows and culled heifers who, with just thirty or forty-five days on feedlot rations, might catch the eye of an order buyer at the sale barn commissioned to bid in for hamburger. Most of them will stay five or six months at the outside and leave as low Choice beef. They will spend their last days of gluttony in one of hundreds of small feeding pens, a hundred or more of them per pen, wallowing in their own excrement and gorging twice a day on the man-made rations of grain and supplements that are dumped by the ton in the concrete feed bunks at the end of each pen. Sickness, disease, and death are the only reprieves from monotony in the final rush to fatness.

Weak, exhausted, and emotionally strained from the long

overland journey by truck, many of the newcomers develop pneumonia or shipping fever and never recover. Those who start healthy rarely stay that way, for the feedlot is really a ghetto, albeit a well-fed one. Cows and heifers who entered the feedlot pregnant miscarry. The more gluttonous heifers suffer prolapsis: their uteruses pop out and hang, pink and bloody,

like large balloons from their hindquarters. Some steers pop their anuses. Other steers somehow excite their neutered pen-mates and are ridden until their backs break. The dried ground cover of dirt and manure, inhaled, causes respiratory diseases. Abscesses and infections arise from crowding and scraping at the feed bunks and along the pen fences. Acidosis is common. Fermentation in the rumen goes awry, and alcohol manufactured to absorb it causes drunken stumbling.

Once or twice a day, hired feedlot cowboys who punch timeclocks and take coffee breaks ride through the pens on horseback, looking for the sickest animals, the ones with snotty noses, bloodshot eyes, stumbling gaits, prolapsis, symptoms of labor. These cattle are cut from the others and herded into the wide alleys that run between the rows of pens. The alleys are carpeted with the decomposing remains of stillborn calves, some bleached white, others nothing more than black, sun-baked balls of rot. Limping and wheezing, the ailing are driven one by one to the hospital pens where the cowboys, assisted by wetbacks, cajole them into a squeeze chute for doctoring. Battery-powered thermometers are rammed into rectums, vitamins and antibiotics shot into flanks or mainlined into arteries in the neck, sulfa boluses the size of golf balls rammed down throats with fifteen-inch tweezers, abscesses lanced of quarts of milky pus with pocketknives and cleansed with a garden hose, prolapsed uteruses crudely shoved back in place and stitched in with heavy surgical thread. If the treatments work, they will prolong the age of gluttony; if they don't, the feedlot's projected annual loss rate will not be significantly affected. Nor will its profits.

There are feedlot cowboys who punch timeclocks and take coffee breaks but neither ride horses nor handle cattle. Some of them spend their days in the feed mill superintending the cooking, grinding, and flaking of the sweet, syrupy rations. Others

drive trucks in which twenty-thousand-pound loads of the final mixture of corn, milo, hay, molasses, urea, cottonseed oil, and chemicals are transported to the concrete feed bunks. These cowboys never taste the rank air of the pens, never hear the symphony of explosive cattle farts and cascading urine. In the feed mill, it is the hissing of the steam plant and the hot roar of the gigantic iron flaking rollers that numb the senses, the vomitous sweetness of the freshly cooked rations that fills the nostrils. And in the feed trucks, it is the whirring of the dumping motors, the flies that upholster the cab, the swirling clouds of corn dust and dirt. But in everyone's eyes is the same evidence: they've all inhaled the smell of money at one time or another. Only the vocabulary of sensation is different.

HARVEST NOTE

October. Corn and milo harvest in full swing. Whining drone of grain driers from two elevators in town. They run all night. Custom cutting crews in town in force. Convoys of grain trucks, headers in beds, combines on trailers pulled behind, often a mobile trailer or van in the rear. Grain trucks parked all around town, especially around the Spa Hotel. At the cafe in the morning, service is slow because of extra customer demand from cutter crews. Cutters wear heavy, insulated monkey suits, boots, seed caps. They come up from southern Texas, work their way to Montana. Talk at the liars' table about yields, mechanical problems with combines. Bell housings, bearings, clutches, axles. Where's that damn Moon? Need some welding down south.

The newly drilled wheat is bright green peach fuzz on the bleached, brown soil. In adjacent fields, drying corn and milo. The milo is burnt amber. Oddball plants stick up across the fields like errant periscopes. The once-verdant rows of corn are whitish yellow. After weeks of drying in the field, each plant sags on one brittle leg. The pleasing regularities of the land are gone, the symmetry of a good crop marred, the neatness of the rowing obscured.

On October 12, Oakley Dorn brings in the first load of corn to the Bartlett elevator. Dennis James delivers the first load of milo. The county newspaper runs a big headline: MILO, CORN HARVEST GETS STARTED IN COUNTY.

The combines, giant prehistoric beasts, lumber from field to field. Red-and-white Internationals, yellow-and-green Deeres, silver Allis Gleaners, military tanks with glassed-in cabs instead of turrets and giraffe-neck unloading augers instead of mounted repeating guns. In front, nine prehensile claws, rocketlike prongs that extend across eight rows of corn during cutting. In the fields, the nine-pronged header assaults the corn stalks, its gnashing, whirring teeth of chains and pulleys violently jerking down the brittle, dehydrated plants. The chains grab the ears and discard the stalks, and the ears are augered into the machine's gullet, there to have the grain shaken loose from cob and husk. Sieves and walkers and blowers move the grain to the bin; the cobs and husks and trash out the back and onto the field. The beasts lumber forward, filling the air with a deafening drone.

Timing. Beat the rain, beat the cold, pick and shell the grain before it gets so dry it blows to the ground. Every piece of equipment, every grain cart and bobtail truck and combine must function flawlessly. The cost of being down is measured in thousands of dollars. Don't get sick. Don't run a loaded truck into the ditch. Don't drink. Don't smoke in the fields or near the elevators.

Unloading on the go at night during corn harvest. A crystal-clear evening. The Milky Way a stream of snowflakes across the black dome. Warm Miller's beer in bottles and sardines and white bread for supper. Combine's headlights illuminating corn rows in front of gnashing teeth of header. Tractor pulling grain cart running parallel on left, bouncing and heaving, taking corn from combine bin via unloading auger. Home to bed at ten. Back in the fields at seven the next morning.

Fingers torn off. Trucks tipping over. Stories. Art Buxton standing on top of old wheat in his elevator, shoveling. There is a cavity; it gives, and Art falls through, sinking to his chest, then his neck. Ten-year-old son Tommy runs for help. They need someone young and strong, not too heavy, to jump in and shovel. Al the Cowman's nephew is not big, but rodeoing has built up his body. He shovels harder and faster than he ever imagined possible, but it doesn't help much. Art keeps sinking. They hook ropes around his wrists and try to hoist him. No good. The grain is up to his nose, and he's spitting and screaming for air. Al the Cowman's nephew shovels faster. They put a hose in Art's mouth and run it outside to the cool night air. No good. Art's lungs collapse from the weight of the wheat. It is the most frightening night in Al's nephew's life.

At dusk, the sunset in the west is predominantly orange, dashes of pink here and there on the horizon. A brume hangs over the flat land, close to the ground: it is composed of dust thrown up by harvesting equipment, plus grain dust from the driers and combines . . . a delicate haze.

4 ❧ Woman's Place

A son's a son till he takes a wife,
A daughter's a daughter all her life.

Old school rhyme recalled by a retired county schoolteacher

Patience. Lots of patience.

Winner's explanation of what it took to win Farm Wife of 1974 award in county

I'm twenty-one, but I feel old. Something like forty. I guess I've just got in the routine of being a housewife. I need to do something irresponsible. Maybe some day I'll take off to Kansas and go swimming.

A county housewife

Mary Sanders: Like in a Jail Sometimes

My dream when I was little was to go to the mountains to live on a ranch. I thought, boy, just to live in the mountains on a ranch'd be something. But if you're raised on a farm, more than likely a farmer's what you're going to be. So I always figured I'd stay right here. You know. They'd do something that'd hold us back. Sure enough. Here I am. (She laughs.)

The grinding of pickup wheels on gravel warns us that Alan Sanders is home from the fields. Mary jumps into action, and dinner preparation begins. The two older Sanders girls embrace their father. He spies the tape recorder, cradles the girls, and without further ado proceeds to interview himself concerning plummeting commodity prices and spiraling farm costs. I feel trapped. Civility requires that I allow Alan to sound off, but I really ought to help Mary with dinner preparations. Mary, however, shoos me out of the kitchen. "He's the one you ought to be interviewin', anyway. I don't have anything to say."

Two hours later, after dinner has been served and the dishes washed up, the girls are put down for naps and Alan returns to the fields. Mary and I sit quietly in the living room of the Sanders' double-wide trailer on the prairie. Once again Mary insists she has nothing interesting to say.

I planned on going to business school. But then I got engaged, and that's all I could think about. We met at a basketball game. He'd just come home from the service and he'd only been home a few days. I really wasn't that much to go out. I had the privilege of takin' the family car to town to drag Main, and I never was really lookin' for a ride. But we got acquainted, and after that we just got hooked. (She laughs.) We had a nice courtship. He was always a gentleman. So I canceled going to school and got married. Which I do wish I would've went ahead with it, because I see now if something would happen to him, I wouldn't have nothin' to go back on. Which I didn't stop to think of at the time. I enrolled and this engagement come up, and that's all I could think about. Love. (She laughs.)

Do you like cooking?

I don't mind it really, 'cause if I didn't have to do that, I don't know what I'd do. This is my responsibility, that I always have a hot meal. Feed my family. It's just about a twenty-four-hour shift. And I've seen some farm women, they just don't care. They don't care if their husband has a hot meal or a bologna sandwich. I feel if the man goes out and works, makes a living for the family, I feel he should be fed good three times a day. I've seen some girls, right

in this community, they'll run to town and buy hamburger for dinner and for supper, and that's all they eat. And I don't think any working man can work on that. It's not a balanced meal.

And I'm glad I have my family to take care of. Sure wouldn't want nothin' to happen to 'em. I'm glad the good Lord give me my girls, didn't take 'em. But I feel like I'm just like in a jail sometimes. I get tired of being cooped up here, day in and day out. It gets kinda old. It's like the same routine. Every morning you get up and take care of the kids. Cook breakfast, and then you cook dinner. Every day, it's the same thing. Which is different if you're outside. Maybe one day you'll be on a tractor, and it'd be something different once in a while. And you're not enclosed all the time. I even like to get out and mow weeds. Just anything to get out of the house.

What's your typical day like?

I get up about five and feed the baby. Then somewhere around six, well, I start breakfast. And then I get breakfast over with, and then it's bathtime for the baby and then pick up things. Wash. Start dinner and get it over with. Maybe iron. Go to town for parts or take something to the field. We usually eat supper around eight or eight-thirty in the summer and five or five-thirty in the winter. I put the kids to bed about eight-thirty, and then I do things I can't do when he's around: mend, sweep, fiddle around. I don't know.

You read in these farm magazines where families, they get out, and they all work together. Well, I've never had the opportunity, 'cause I've always had these little ones and always somebody to cook for. I shouldn't feel that way, 'cause I love my kids, but still, it's a feeling that I think everybody has. They like to have a little freedom, you know, away from the daily routine.

The baby cries, waking the other children. Mary rocks the four-month-old in her arms. The three-year-old watches the color television in the living room. Mary is nervous about talking in front of the five-year-old. "She's old enough to understand." I devise a coloring game for the five-year-old to work on in the kitchen. For a few moments, there is peace.

I just don't know how to explain how I feel. There's just times that I'd like to be off by myself, be able to do something that I really want to do and not have to hurry to get it done so I can get back and get started on something else. That's how I feel. If I could go out and do something outside without having to worry about, "Well, I've got to get back in and get dinner started by so and so."

I like to sew, but I just sew to mend now. I don't get time to set down and sew like I like to, 'cause when I sit down to sew, I want to sew and nothin' else. I don't want nothing or nobody interfering, so I can concentrate on what I'm doing. You can't do that with kids 'cause it's either "Mom, I've got to go potty," or, "Mom, I want a cookie." And if I'm going to do something, I want to sit down and do it and enjoy it and not just do a few stitches here and put it up for the week.

He always depends on me to always have a hot meal, 'cause he never has a cold dinner unless I have to take one of the kids to the doctor or something like that. Other than that, he always has a hot meal waitin' on him. If he's going to eat, I tell him come in and eat while it's hot instead of having to have it warmed up two and three times. I tell 'im how I feel, because it's my job to have it done and if he don't respect what I have done, then it makes me darn good and mad. Just like coming in today at twelve-thirty. There's no reason that he had to work thirty minutes late. He can come in for dinner at twelve and then go back. But he gets busy, he forgets, and he don't think about me. When we have a late dinner like that, then it messes up my whole afternoon. I'm late getting the dishes done, and I've got things that I've got to do, and he don't stop to think that I have my job to do in the house, and it messes up my whole day.

I'm always wanting someone to talk to. If I get lonely, I've got the girls, but that's not like talkin' to someone to express your ideas, your values. I think it's good to have someone you can talk to, tell 'em your troubles. Cry on their shoulder. Instead of keeping it all bottled up. A group of women, they all tell their troubles. He's not much on how he feels. He don't say too much. He's got maybe something bothering him, he don't come out with it. If I have something bothering me, I'm going to tell him, to get it over with. I think it makes a person feel better.

He just kind of takes advantage. That's my feeling. He just kind of figures, "Well, I know she'll have it hot for me when I get there." I get kinda discouraged, 'cause I know he doesn't think about it. Maybe I'm just an old gripe, but he'll come in with his muddy shoes. Cow manure on my rug. Why don't he slip 'em off on the outside instead of bringing all that mud up in the house? He's always got clean clothes. He never has to wear dirty clothes. He don't stop to think, 'cause he comes in, and he's hot, and he's tired, and he's hungry. But I've seen it if he goes to another person's house, boy, he scrapes his feet off.

Hi and bye. That's about all we get to say to each other. It's kind of good to be just together. Watch TV or just being together in the same room is a lot, because we don't get to be like that too often when there's three kids, and the TV's blarin', and maybe he's not even home half the time. It's kinda good to have him sittin'.

I guess I've got a lifetime of cooking ahead of me. I'm sure we'll always farm, and we've got three kids that'll be home for quite a few years. And it's possible there might be one on the way right now. I just kinda hope I ain't, 'cause it's hard to have 'em both so young. But that's what you get for givin' in just once. (She laughs.) Bingo.

Do you think you'll ever leave? Get that mountain ranch?

(She shakes her head.) We've always been here, so this is all we know. It's a pretty good living, I guess. Like he says, we're not wealthy, but we've got plenty to eat and plenty of clothes to wear. So I guess it's the main thing. And we're happy. (She laughs.) I don't know. Can you imagine just going to town and not having to worry about anything? Just buy anything you wanted and not have to worry about where it's going to come from?

I wonder what they mean by equal. I have all the freedoms I want. I can go any place I want just like anybody else. He's never treated me mean. I have the checkbook. I have the privilege to go buy whatever I feel like I need, which isn't too often because we've got to count our dollars. I'm equal to that. I couldn't ask for anything better. But I think a man, they feel like they've got the go-ahead. The woman's always kind of stood in the background and kinda, what the man says, fine. I think it's always been like that. And I don't know if it'll ever change or not.

VOIDS

I call Denise Wright to see if I can drop by her trailer home to run the tape recorder, but instead I get invited to a Fashion Two-Twenty party. When I arrive at two, she comes out to greet me. Stan is cutting corn, and the first thing Denise says is how lonely she's been, what with harvest on and Stan not coming in till nine or ten at night. Inside, I meet Denise's mother (western-cut pantsuit, bleached blond hair piled high). Judy Jones (peach-colored pantsuit) and Erma Simpson (blue pantsuit) from church are there. A little later, one of Mrs. Green's married granddaughters-in-law comes in. What would I like to drink? The choice is Kool Aid or Pepsi. There are cookies and brownies. The women talk about cooking and hairdos, but inevitably in connection with their husbands' preferences. The husbands are never referred to by name. It is always "him" or "he." Denise is hostess, and at three o'clock she spreads the products out on the kitchen table. Oohs and ahs. There's Angel Blue Eye Shadow and Emerald Green Eye Shadow, Moisturizer, Eye-and-Throat Lotion, Freshener, Tahitian Shade Magic Stick, Blending Rouge, Mystic Blush, Lip Sleek, Lip Liner, Lip Gloss, Zing Bath Oil, Perfume Milk Bath, Formula 19 Pre-Makeup Base, Dusting Powder. The ladies remove lids, sniff scents, shade colors onto forearms. How do you keep eye shadow from caking? You use this new cream base and spread it on before you put on the eye shadow. Denise announces it is time to order. Or does somebody want a facial? Nobody volunteers. It's getting late. We fill out order forms, and I select two eye shadows: Mystic and Jolly Green. Denise persuades me to try the Formula 19 also. My bill comes to seven dollars, half the next smallest in the group. Denise studies the booklet of free gifts to which, as hostess, she might have been entitled if there'd been a larger turnout. She sighs. It was just a spur-of-the-moment idea. She needed the distraction.

There are three beauty shops in this town, and when I first come down here, I thought, "Oh dear, it'll probably be all I can do to make a living." But you'd be surprised at the business there is. If you have the right touch, you can talk 'em into anything. They want to look nice. When they get their hair done, they want to appeal to somebody: their husband, the lady next door. To appeal is the only reason they're here. But we are definitely the last ones to get in on the newer hairdos. As far as fashion and trend is concerned, back-combing is out. Throughout the country, it's no teasing, no back-combing. Very casual. Something that's easy to take care of and everything. But I cannot convince my ladies. Here, it's back-combing and hair spray and "Make it look stiff!" But it's not only their hair, it's beauty, period. And they don't care what it costs. Say I've got a new product. They're willing to buy it and try it. In the city, people were kinda hesitant. It was all I could do to get a lady to buy a thing of make-up. But women here will buy anything, I don't know why. Maybe if they don't have access to it, they're gonna try. I don't know.

I am trying to understand and describe these women. It is difficult for me to be sympathetic. It is difficult for me to see individuals. Lives and faces merge, and all I see are stereotypes. Every morning, year in and year out, the stereotype rises at 6:30 A.M. *in her little stucco bungalow in town, fixes breakfast for the children, sees him off to the fields or the cafe, dresses the youngest children for school in between starting a load of laundry and scraping toast crusts into the sink. And starts to feel that ineffable something between dread and anticipation that presages the solitude and quiet that always descend at eight-fifteen, when the last child has been hustled off to school and the washing machine sputters to a stop. Her life is so different from Mama's. He does not consult her the way Daddy did with Mama. She's never even looked at the farm books. And with a hired hand, he doesn't require her occasional service in the fields. He isn't the most patient man in the world: there'd be sharp words for sure if they were out there branding and sorting cows together. Besides, even if she worked with him outside all day, she'd still have all the work to do at home. He isn't the kind of man to come home and say, "Well, since you've worked, we'll run down to the cafe for supper."*

Mama and Daddy did everything together, and Mama used to worry about the crops and the prices as much as Daddy did. Now, the men down at the cafe know that he has rented some new land or ripped up a maize field before she does. Of course, she still feels the pressure of the agricultural calendar. Harvesttime, her cooking duties double, triple. Twice a day she loads the family station wagon with meat, vegetable, and salad plates and drives to the fields to feed him and the custom cutters. Twice a day, she drives home and scrubs the cutlery and Tupperware and plastic. Make no doubt about it, she's proud to be a farmer's daughter, and she's proud to be a farmer's wife. But she's not hankering to be a farmer. When you've grown up in the country, you've earned your right to solitude and leisure, that's all. You'd never go back. You've grown enough gardens, candled enough pullet eggs, worried about enough hail storms, and jerked on enough milk cow tits to last you a lifetime.

The closest these gals have ever been to beauty is a magazine. They don't have big department stores where you have your regular cosmetics and a gal that's trained to tell you how this blush goes on. There's a lot of them, farmers' wives, that have worked right out there alongside the man growing up or even in the first married years. A lot of them are getting older, and they have a bit more time on their hands. Their husbands are saying, "Go get your hair done." They are a little bit more prosperous. They've never had time for themselves, and they're finally getting time for their hair, their complexion. Until harvest is over, they kinda watch their Ps and Qs on their money, but after harvest, when you know they've got money coming in, they'll come in once a week.

Sometimes, I imagine this woman I seek to describe must feel voids closing in around her like big, black rollers. She has thought about working at the variety store. Or maybe using the typing she learned years ago in high school. Or going back to school. But how? There aren't office jobs around, and the nearest college campus is miles away. There isn't even a factory nearby for part-time work. It must help having Mama and sisters and friends down the street. It must help having club on Friday where you can learn to sew pants that really fit, or roll bandages and visit the shut-ins. It must help having Bible study classes and bridge games and catalogs.

Catalogs. She window-shops in her living room by thumbing the latest ones. She checks the racks at Town Variety when they put up the semiannual "Everything Reduced" sign. She reads the ladies magazines, too, but there's really no substitute for checking out the styles firsthand. The most exquisite interludes are those visits to shopping malls and plazas hours away, where the fabulous variety of styles and fabrics and colors may be eyed and touched and tried on.

Everything has to be a game, a party, and I myself always

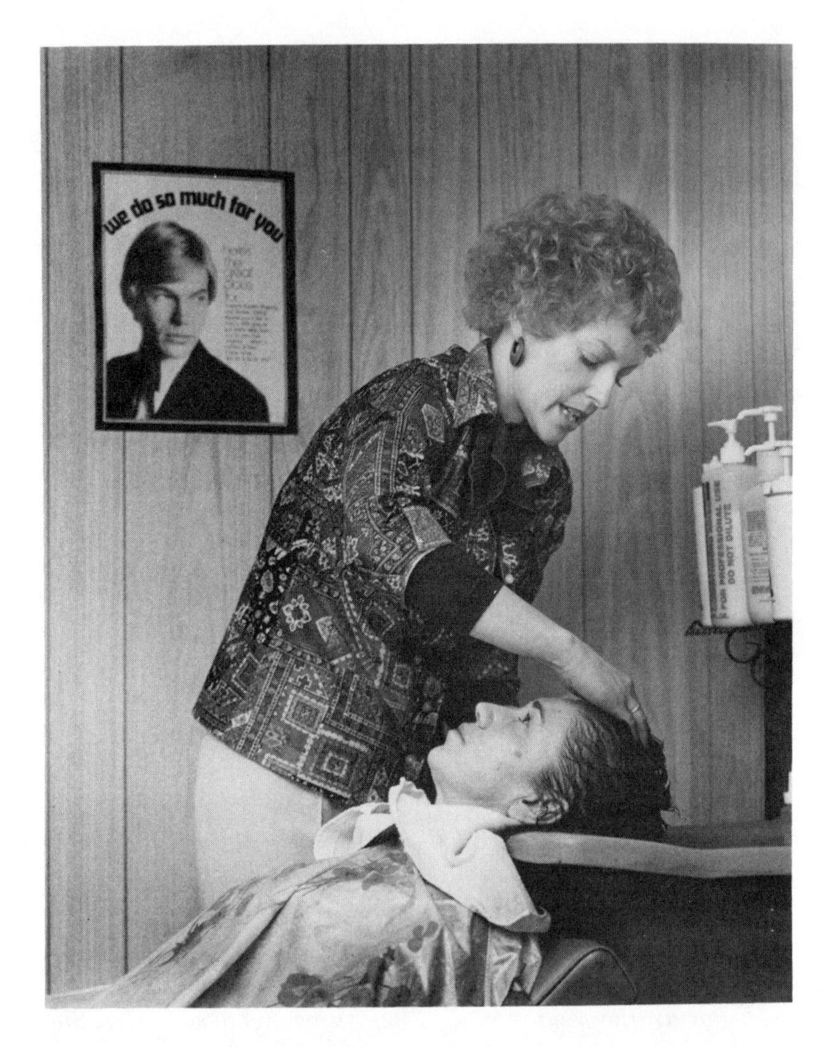

feel ugly, out of place, uptight. At my first Tupperware party, the hostess serves pistachio cake, brownies, coffee, and soft drinks. We sit in a circle in the living room and look through the order book, take forms. The hostess opens up the suitcase of wares in the middle of the room and lays them out neatly. Orange, lemon, avocado, and clear collections, plain lids and fluted lids. Cake holders, containers, juice jugs, pitchers, pie plates, dishes, pans, bread boxes. The hostess passes a bowl filled with party favors, and I take a coffee measuring spoon. Then we play a game. What side of an English tea cup is the handle on? (The outside.) What is the first thing you do when you fall in the lake? (Get wet.) Which is correct, 9 and 6 are 17, or 9 and 6 is 17? (Neither.) Then we order. Everyone is building sets, and there is great excitement about new additions.

Women have always told me that if they want to relax and let loose and just forget about everything for a couple of hours, they go to the beauty shop. A hairdresser might as well have a psychologist's license. Instead of a hydraulic chair, we need a couch. I've heard everything from children and school problems to so-and-so's running around with so-and-so. Some of them think they're being mistreated, because their husband doesn't get home till late at night, and here they have supper waiting for 'em. Or their husbands went out of town today on business or something, had to get a water pump, and didn't come back, or if they did come back, they were loaded. Or they feel like they're being tied down. They'll just come in and blow off a little steam and leave feeling great. I guess instead of a hairdresser, you'd call me a listening friend.

Maybe this stereotype of a woman dreamed of being a model. Like at the fashion shows during county fair, having everyone watch you sashay across the stage in an elegant outfit: perfect figure, perfect posture. They rig up the auditorium so it looks just like Miss America: mock Roman columns and canopied stairs and long ramps with little electric bulbs on the border, music and a master of ceremonies. But instead of modeling or going to beauty school or doing a year at business college, she married him. That was the pinnacle of her existence: the gown, the flowers, the attention, the pictures in the county newspaper. She doesn't look at her wedding album anymore, but for the first few years she and her girlfriends did just that when they got together.

Children change all that. You become a wife at sixteen or seventeen, a mother nine months later, a grandmother at thirty-five and a great-grandmother well before sixty. Sowing and reaping. Mary is expecting, Opal is due in June. Births are listed weekly on the front page of the county newspaper. Doc Pete has fifteen mothers due in the last two weeks of August. A cousin or niece gets pregnant, and maternity clothes break loose and work their way out through the branches of the family tree.

Her job is to bear and nourish, to cope with the terrible twos, to wash with soap and vinegar mouths that discover naughty words, to attend parent-teacher conferences, to let the superintendent know when there's too much homework or rumors about a new teacher's nightlife. He may be at her side when Johnny makes the starting team, but not when Susie's candles take first prize at the home-ec sale. And although in the first few courting months he may have squired her to church functions and vowed in the back seat of the car to become the family's spiritual head, it is her duty to escort the little ones to Sunday school and Bible school, a Sisyphean enterprise it so often turns out at puberty when sons and headstrong daughters fall into his backsliding ways.

During the day, after the pickup's pulled out, or at night, after he has fallen asleep in the recliner in front of the television, there is cleaning. Daily cleaning, weekly cleaning, seasonal cleaning, special cleaning after dust storms. There's always so much dust. And sewing and ironing and mending. And cooking, Lord is there cooking: always breakfast and a hot noon meal for the children and the possibility that he, accus-

tomed all his life to demand feeding, will surprise her and come in from the fields early, late, or not at all.

Where, I sometimes wonder, has all the romance gone? It's plain. Into shopping in town and fetching the mail; into visits with the Avon lady and children and sales; into crinoline and organdy dresses and pastel curtains and porcelain figurines; into cooking and cleaning and diapers and detergents; television, prayer meetings, velveteen divans and wall-to-wall shag; muddy boots in the foyer and blood-spattered branding jeans in the hamper; overcooked meat and lard on the griddle.

Marla Stutz: Stand Up and Kick a Little Ass

She is poised and attractive, married now to a wealthy local farmer's son who, born in the county but raised in a faraway city, has returned to the town to pursue his own ambivalent version of the agrarian dream. Like Mike Klimm, she seeks us out before we even know she exists, riding up to the law office one morning on her bicycle, wearing a tie-dyed T-shirt. As the tape recorder rolls, she breathlessly pours out her life's story. This proves to be the first of many long, cathartic sessions.

I was raised on the farm. My mother said that milking cows would make my fingers strong for playing the piano. I raised sheep to show in fairs. I worked for neighbors driving tractors, and that's how I paid for some of my college. The work that I contributed was outdoors work, in the fields. At home I just had to make the beds and wash the supper dishes. So I had a pretty easy childhood. Pretty spoiled.

My mother had to scrub floors for a living. I mean, she can work like any man in the world. And she always said,

"You'll never scrub a floor." She wanted her daughter to be all the things in the world she wasn't. She wanted to be a ballerina, and she always wanted to play the piano. There were no ballet teachers around; but there were piano teachers, so I got piano lessons. My mother didn't want me to be a common, ordinary down-home-type person. She didn't teach me how to sew, even though she's an excellent seamstress. Instead of learning how to cook, I learned to sing. I don't know if she even wanted me to be a mother per se. I think she wanted me to be way up there doing things. So I didn't have to do a damn thing growing up. Just read and get out was the message I got. She never said that in so many words and she'd deny it if you asked her, but she always encouraged it in subtle ways. She wanted me to be something different.

A high school romance with a neighboring farm boy nearly canceled her mother's wishes. "His program was that he'd go to the Army, and I'd go to school and get my degree and be a teacher. We'd come home and live half a mile from the school and live happily ever after." But her mother enrolled her in a summer school program after graduation and then pushed her on to college. "They had to drag me out the door. My mother said, 'You're going.' And my boyfriend was on the phone, and I'm crying, and my dad says, 'She doesn't have to go.' But my mother said, 'She's going.' So I went, and the romance that was supposed to last forever lasted half of a day." When she talks about her college years, she smokes many cigarettes. She is alternately nostalgic and bitter.

College was traumatic in terms of the academic world. My grades weren't too hot, and I got into all types of trouble. I was threatened by the dean many times. I drank a lot. I was nasty to my dorm mother. I think I rebelled against every rule that was ever written. I wasn't on probation, but I thought the time was drawing nigh. (She laughs.) So I decided to quit school, went home and got a job. Then I switched to a junior college-type place. It was pretty much kids from rural areas or city kids that couldn't make it. They weren't really much different from what I was.

I think if I'd been more prepared academically I wouldn't have been so destructive, but I was badly discouraged. I thought I knew so much, you know, had a good education in high school, and that was a joke. I had no education. Even in my best subjects I had problems. I took a literature class, I don't remember what it was, but they were so far ahead of what I had. I couldn't even keep up, and I read fast, but most of them had read a lot of this before. They're reading Shakespeare, and to them this was nothing new, but all I had had was *Julius Caesar* in ninth grade. And they would go into Greek mythology, all the different gods and how they're related. Everybody knew all these little hierarchies, and I didn't even know what it was. And like the library. (She laughs.) We had to write a term paper for psychology class, and this woman said to check in the periodical room. I had to look in the dictionary to see what periodical meant. (She laughs.) I took this German class, you know, and it was really a scream. I found out I didn't even know English grammar, so how in hell could I take a German class? That's when I switched to elementary education. That was the easy way out.

It was even worse than I'm telling you. I don't take defeat lightly, and it was very depressing. I used my social life to escape. I would sit and admire the kids that could sit around and study and were not pseudo-intellectuals, but real intellectuals. I admired them so much, but I never fit in, because I didn't understand what they were talking about. I don't know who I hung around with. A lot of them never came back the second year. That was the group. What would you call them, flunkies or something?

I would never trade my college experience for anything. I would just do it differently. I loved school, and I'd love to go back. I'd go tomorrow, I really would, just to try to start over and pay attention. But it's too late.

After college, she took off alone to a large city and worked her way up to a responsible position in a stock brokerage company. "I took a lot of college workshops, learned a lot, met a lot of fascinating people. I fit right in, and people were always surprised to learn I was from a small farm town out here." Then she got married and had a child. Her husband left her when the child was three months old. "I had the baby when I was twenty-nine years old, and I didn't know how to take care of him. I know that sounds ridiculous for a farm girl, but I didn't know how to take care of him." She came back home and lived with her parents. After a listless couple of years, she met her present husband and remarried.

I swallowed a lot of pride coming back. I had rolled out of here in such high fashion. A couple of people said, "Well, we didn't expect for *you* to be back here." I don't know why I wanted my boy to be raised on a farm. I saw what the kids in the city do, and it's so different from what you see as a child on the farm. Concepts are different. Values are different. I lived in some rotten neighborhoods in the city. I wasn't in the financial situation to go back to the city and have him in a beautiful open-air day-care center. I thought about open spaces. Here, my boy sees caterpillars making cocoons to be butterflies. He's really understanding a lot of the stuff that he's seeing. Cows having calves. He's seen life, and he's seen death. He counted cows this morning, and he counted thirty-two and a half cows and one dead one. I suppose people in the city see life and death, but I think they see it with people getting shot or something maybe. My boy can run across the yards and fields and really have freedom.

But there are a lot of things about a small town like this that frustrate me. I can't communicate with a lot of people. I don't confide in anyone but my new husband. We're together a lot. We're together more than two invalids. (She laughs.) I've found out through the couple of things I've gotten involved with here that I'm just better off doing my own thing. I'm just too damned abrasive. I upset people. If I'm worked up about something, I just start spouting off. I can't keep my mouth shut.

What do you think of woman's lot here?

Women in these small communities are so damned suppressed it makes me sick to my stomach sometimes. Clean

the house, wash the car. Barefoot and pregnant-type thing. Have you ever driven around with a farmer? I remember my mother telling my father he was as worthless as the tits on a boar because he'd drag her to town, and she'd sit there for like eight hours while he'd go to one shop after another. Visiting with his friends. Then he'd hop back in the pickup. And there's the little wife sitting there. And they'd go somewhere else, and he'd get out and talk and talk, about who knows what. But there's no consideration about this person sitting out in this hot pickup waiting for him to take her home. They never say they're sorry. Why not? Because women don't stand up and kick a little ass.

I think the men are insecure. This person told me that her husband hit her one day. She didn't even seem particularly alarmed about it. She said, "He came home, and the kids had been sick, and I was just behind schedule, and I didn't have dinner on the table, and he said, 'I have been out in the fields since five-thirty this morning, so the least you can do is have my dinner ready for me.'" And hits her. Now I can't quite put it together. Does she say, "Get your own food, Charlie, I'm hopping off"? Or does she say, "You're right, dear; I am wrong because I haven't held up my end of the stick"?

I guess it's just a matter of having some respect. I don't think the women have respect for their husbands. They fear them. And the men have zero respect for their wives, because their wives fear them. What's the old story? I, the woman, am seven things: the wife, the mistress, the lover, the house cleaner, the toilet cleaner. . . . I'm supposed to be all these things. But women aren't anything to themselves. They don't have a great deal of respect for themselves. They don't fight back, and I think they're jealous of people who do. Men don't accept women as people here.

I've been in situations where this woman has fixed this huge meal for all these people—like at these family dinners—and the men will sit in their chairs and say, "GET ME A PIECE OF PIE." You know, "Get me a piece of pie." (She laughs.) They don't ever say, "Please." Maybe that's something I shouldn't resent. But here she has worked her rear end off, it's a vacation day, and she's told to get up and get a piece of pie. And she does it. (She pauses.) She does it.

There's just so many things that I love about the country, and there's so many things I miss about the city. I don't know that we'll stay here forever. I just keep saying, "Is this what you're going to do the rest of your life? Is this where you want to be?" I ask myself that every day. I'd like to work or go back to school. I'd like to work at an interesting job. Not necessarily teaching school or working in a variety store. I'd like to try working in a drug or alcoholic rehabilitation center. Or something to do with child abuse. I'd like to play tennis every day. I'd just like to keep learning something. I wish there was something here where people could get together as a group and learn something.

I think man is just basically a dissatisfied creature. I don't think I'm unusual in that sense. I know I'm capable of doing a number of things. But I don't do 'em. I just sort of sit and while away time. Accomplishment is that self-satisfaction I feel, like if I take a good picture or read a book I really enjoy and discuss it with somebody. Or watch my son grow, and his accomplishments. Sometimes even cooking something that tastes good, 'cause I didn't know how to cook and that's a challenge to me. But keeping house or ironing or decorating doesn't represent accomplishment.

Basically, I'm not so dissatisfied that I'm stomping and

walking the floor. I'm sure things could be so much worse. I have more freedom now than I've ever had in my life. I have no restrictions. I have money to spend. Just something is missing.

CHRISTIAN WIVES

Several times a year, in groups of five to ten, Christian ladies go to school. They order the course materials—programmed study guides, study books, cassettes—and meet once a week at each other's homes. The courses last ten weeks at the most, and each one is different; so it is possible to take several each year. Groups are formed on the basis of family and friendship, and with a mixing of faiths: Baptist, Friends, Church of Christ, even a Methodist or two. Refreshments are served after each session of listening to the tape-recorded Voice.

Click.
Whrrrrr.
Voice.

Good morning, ladies. Our first lesson is God's plan for men. Our scripture is 1 Corinthians 13:7. Beareth all things, believeth all things, hopeth all things, endureth all things.

We start with Genesis. God creates man. Puts in man his drives. To exercise dominion, subdue, multiply, tend, guard. That is, lead, control, procreate, provide, protect. Woman God's love gift to man. Companion. Helper. Concept of femininity obsolete? Liberationists right? No. Woman's arms curved for child-cradling. Man's strong back. And archaeological evidence. The hunt. No women. Less aggressive, can't throw, get lost. So your husband's bad traits really God-given drives. Works too much? Subduing. Sex crazy? Admonished to multiply. Overly protective? Guarding territory. Compliment when leads. Don't correct in public. Catch self when want to win argument. Reconsider when attempt task he can do better. Ask yourself each day: are you helping to build your husband's ego in God's image?

Click.

Plates of blueberry cobbler are passed around. Diets and resolutions to diet are mentioned, then violated. Naughty laughter and excitement. Gossip. Did you know that Linda Higgins is expecting? Really? That was fast. Well, Loretta Nordway was faster. Susan came home from school with the news that three seniors are pregnant. Is that a fact? Who? Is your niece going to marry my nephew? I don't know. Her mother wishes she had the answer to that question, too. Carol, what's the recipe for this cobbler? It's just delicious. It is. Mmmmmmmm. Well, it's almost noon. Better get home and get dinner on the table.

Click.

Whrrrr.

Voice.

Good morning, ladies. This morning's lesson is submission. Our scripture is Colossians 3:18. Wives, submit yourselves unto your own husbands, as it is fit in the Lord.

Close your eyes and remember your wedding day. You gave up your individuality to become a wife. Cannot submit to Christ till submit to husband. An attitude, a belief, a conviction. God's way. And many rewards. Security. Freedom from decisions. Joy of daily chores. Of course, even if husband requests, no idolatry, no adultery, no witchcraft, no murder. But decline in a submissive manner.

Click.

The snack at Glena's is tunnel of fudge cake. Is this dietetic? Dream on. Do you watch television with Orville? I can't stand those football games. Me either. For the life of him, Alvis will not read. And I love to read. I love to read also. But they want you with them in front of the TV. I sit there and look but I couldn't tell you what was going on. My mind is a million miles away. Well, Odus doesn't care if I sit with him, but he sure has me running back and forth bringing things to him while he sits there.

When she gets angry, Velma scrubs her bathroom as hard as she can. Cleaning out closets pacifies Anna Ray. With three daughters at Glena's house, there's always someone going through that time of the month. What is Mary going to do when she graduates? Glena is distraught. Mary doesn't really have anyone right now, and anymore, there's too much college pressure. Opal's daughter knows a girl that began taking beauty courses right out of high school because she didn't know what else to do. Then she decided to become a nurse. She wasted all that time and money in the beauty program. Isn't that a shame?

Click.

Whrrrrr.

Voice.

Hello, ladies. For those of you who have grown up in a Christian home, this lesson is unnecessary. But for the rest, it is necessary to review the God-given principles of parenthood. Our scripture today is Proverbs 13:24. He that spareth his rod hateth his son: but he that loveth him chasteneth him betimes.

At the top of the child-rearing hierarchy is the father. A woman might spend more time with her children, but her husband is accountable to God for them. Watch interfering. You look sad when children are disciplined? Duty to support husband before children. In his absence, carry out commands. Mother second. Handle children in husband's absence. Roll out in morning and fix hot breakfasts? Chauffeur to football and dentist? Dominated by your children? Should be bottom of hierarchy. If children don't obey earthly fathers, how obey Heavenly Father? Give boys masculine tasks. Homosexuality on rise. Long hair, ruffles. Children learn by example.

Click.

Opal, did you make an apple pie? This crust is *so* good. How do you do it? Vinegar and egg? I'll take the recipe. You know, this homosexuality thing is something I've wondered about. It makes me sick simply to think about it. I know. But we're more tolerant today, and I wonder. Is this good? There's more and more of it. I think so. But as Christians, aren't we to love everyone? Even homosexuals? Well, maybe we can love people but not what they do. The devil works in devious ways. Well, look at astrology and all this horoscope business. The devil gets to people and they start accepting things like homosexuality and horoscopes. It scares me. Me too. Just hearing you talk scares me. I don't know about this devil business. Well, just read your Bible. Used to be, worst thing that could happen to your daughter was that she had to get married. I'll consider myself lucky if Beth has just that. I'm terrified she'll get into devil worship or those seances and things. Gives me the creeps.

Carol needs some advice. She's trying to lose weight and now that harvest's on, Pete doesn't get in till nine at night or later. That means he doesn't eat his supper till near ten, and bedtime is less than an hour after that. He gets angry if she doesn't eat with him, but that means she goes to sleep on a full stomach. Should she eat with him and ruin her diet? Or make him mad and hold off? Glena responds. Fix yourself a salad and go ahead and eat with him. Then you can eat your real supper earlier but still make him feel like you're eating with him when he comes home. General consensus and approval. Carol is content.

Click.
Whrrrrr.
Voice.

Good morning, ladies. Our lesson this week is the woman at home. Our scripture is 1 Timothy 5:14. I will therefore that the younger women marry, bear children, guide the house, give none occasion to the adversary to speak reproachfully.

Homemaking is the oldest and most revered profession. So why does the homemaker suddenly find herself under attack? Much skill and creativity in homemaking. Actually, an artist's work. But county fairs no longer emphasize. Nor do schools. Planned by men, career-minded women. So many academic requirements, no room for home economics. Mothers, teach your daughters. Make plans. Avoid same chores every day. Exercise while you clean. Needlepoint breaks for a treat. Shop once a week. Keep frozen salads on hand. Save money and sew clothes, no safety pins. What feels better than making lunches on your own freshly baked bread?

Click.

Oh, I needed that. I get in a rut and do the same things day after day. I like housework. So do I. You sure feel like you've accomplished something when you clean out a closet or get a whole mess of ironing done. My mother was such a good housekeeper; I always feel like a failure compared to her. I need to make plans and shop only once a week. My problem is starting supper a half hour before it's due and finding I'm missing something I need.

Isn't this course helping you? Oh, yes. I find I accept things that used to, I'd get angry over. Well, I talked to Orville about the course. I tell him about each lesson and he likes it. Pete does too. I think Orville is testing me, to see if I really have changed. Oh? Yesterday was the first day he stayed home with me when it was too wet to go to the fields and didn't go out with the boys to the cafe or something. He sat home and watched television. So it's worked. I've been letting him have his way and be the boss, everything the class says, and he doesn't know if it will last, but he really likes it.

I'm going to miss this class. Me too. What I got out of this course is two words: Ask him. I've swallowed my pride and started asking him questions. I do that more, too. Like yesterday, I asked him what we should eat, and he said, and this really surprised me, "You're in a bind, just go up and buy some bologna and we'll have sandwiches." And that was so easy. Well, Ogle and my relationship has changed totally. Even the kids notice their daddy's home more. I've been going with him constantly. I don't know, he wants me along, even when he goes for repairs or something. I can tell the difference too. If he asks me to jump, I say, "How far?"

Ooooooooooh! Whipped cream and angel food. You shouldn't have, Anna Ray. I'll sure miss having something every week. What do you suppose she looks like? Who? The Voice, the woman giving the class. Well, I think she's skinny and blond and looks just the way I want to look. She's one of those perfectly neat women with an immaculate house. I really like her. Me too. I feel like I know her. I wish I had taken this course eighteen years ago when I got married. It sure could have made things smoother. I have an idea. Vina, how about offering the course to our teen-age daughters? This is something we should pass on to our daughters.

Kate Browning: Anything a Man Can Do

Well, I suppose, the life I lead here, I wouldn't live it any other way; so it would probably have been more convenient if I'd have been a man, yes. But I'm not sorry. I haven't had any problem so far. I don't know as things would have been any different. Anyway, I've never wanted to be a man bad enough to go over there and get an operation.

I have found a few farm wives who keep the books, order parts, and call the new four-wheel drive tractor or the new Gleaner M with three-stage separation their "brand-new living room furniture"—not many, but a few. I seek, however, the real woman farmer. Someone suggests Kate Browning up north. The suggestion is accompanied by a wink and an exaggerated fluttering of the right hand. I grab the tape recorder and go. Arriving, I see a small figure near the barn. The figure wears farmer's overalls and a short-sleeved work shirt, a white tennis hat, and wire-rimmed sunglasses. The face is lined and sunburned. The exposed arms and hands are deeply tanned and thick with calluses. The voice is a high, birdlike chirp.

My dad started me farming in the wheat fields before I was five years old, 'cause I started school when I was five, and he started me driving a team of horses that winter. When we came out here in '29, why, he got a tractor, and he put me on the tractor. One brother's two years older than me, and we was young enough they put us two together. We went an hour or two at a time and then we'd change, and my brother that's five years older took his hitch. We drove the tractors that way all day long. My folks started me out young working, and I've never been sorry. I still like to work. I don't like to sit around. But my dad and me, we never did get along. I think he always kinda resented me, 'cause he was always partial to my younger brother and he was always wanting him to get out and go. And my brother never did go. I mean, he just gets along with whatever he's got today. That's all he wants. He didn't like to farm, and it was always kind of a disappointment, I think, to my dad. I'm not braggin' on myself, but I started buying my own land, my own equipment, one thing and another. Never did marry. Never had any desires so far to get married. Never met anybody yet that I thought I'd want to spend the rest of my life with. I've been told the time will come that I'll be sorry I don't have some children, but I don't know. Maybe so. But that time hasn't come yet, anyway. I see some of these people that raise a large family, and when they get old and can't take care of themselves, why the kids don't pay any attention to them. Never go to see them and a few more things. I've got some nieces and nephews that think about as much of me as they do their parents, so maybe they'll take care of me. Maybe I'm just as well off.

She farms with a widowed neighbor, Liz Coates, and a hired hand, Shirley Allen, sometimes taking on hired men or wetbacks. It is July; still some wheat to harvest. Kate goes to town on business and sends Liz and me out to the fields to check a broken-down combine. We are supplied a part and told to install it. Liz wears brown cowboy boots, blue slacks, a large man's shirt. Her hair is close-cropped, and she has a deep smoker's cough. As we bump along pitted county roads, two shotguns on the rack behind us rattle against the window. Kate said we'd see the problem right off, but Liz looks and looks in vain around the unloading mechanism. She mumbles to herself and pokes at the exposed gears and pulleys and belts. At last we notice a naked bolt sticking out of the jumble of combine innards. I get the replacement part and try it. It fits.

I never did like dancing, I don't drink much, and I don't have much religion. I went to church and Sunday school real regular when I was a kid. We used to have lots of picnics and parties and stuff like that, but when I got out of high school, I graduated, I guess, from church also. I always donate to the church. I still believe in it, but I just don't go. I'll tell you one reason I don't go. I don't think I've had a dress on since I got out of high school. And I just don't think that's hardly the place to wear slacks. Dresses was always in the road, and you didn't have enough pockets in them for nothing. I bought me a western suit, and you can just about get in anywhere in slacks, if you've got shoes on.

When I go visiting, it depends on the family. Sometimes I visit with the man, and sometimes with both of them. A lot of times Liz and I are together. She's been farming ever since her husband passed away, and she was raised out here on a farm just like I was. Now that her husband has passed away, we do a lot together. If we go together, she'll visit with the woman, and I'll visit with the man. Most these married women, when they get together, why all they talk about is their kids. I don't have no kids, so I can't talk to them. You take a big percent of married women, that's all they talk about.

Sometimes we go to the city. We have a little trouble finding our way around sometimes, but we're not any dumber than the city folks are when they come down in this country. 'Course, I've never been to New York, and I don't suppose I'll ever go to New York. I just don't like to travel like that. I like to go to the mountains a few days, go fishing and camping and things like that. When I'm up there three or four days, then I'm ready to come home. I go to Lawrence Welk when he comes. I kinda like his music, and I go up there for some of the shows. And I go to the Ice Follies and a few things like that, so I can kinda keep up with the world.

She navigates the pickup along a field road at the downhill end of a newly irrigated corn field to study each furrow for water. Carefully counting the rows, she uses a broken stub of pencil to jot down the numbers of those that haven't watered. Then she backs up, steers for the uphill end of the field, and counts down the rows the same way she did below. She stops by the furrows that have watered and closes the gates on the gated aluminum pipe—no more water for them for a week or two. Then she drives a little farther and opens ten new gates. Watering she doesn't mind, but lifting pipe is beginning to get to her.

A woman can do anything a man can do, so I can't understand how some of these men on the farm let their hair get long. It bothers me. I've always got my hair cut short, ever since I can remember, and it's going to get

shorter than this when I get through cutting wheat, 'cause I'm going to the barber shop. Anymore, men let their hair get long. It's stringy, and the wind blows it, and it catches all the dirt. I don't know how they put up with it.

Do you ever feel you're discriminated against because you're a woman? Any credit problems or things like that?

(She shakes her head.) Nope. The banker has been real good to me. Don't you think it might maybe be the individual? I haven't ever had any problem with credit. I take my turn right along with the men. Now, a lot of times, the men will step back for me to be waited on in front of them, and I don't do that. Other women there, why, they've stepped in front of the men, but I still think everybody ought to take their turn. And I think I've made a lot of friends by doing that. I think they appreciate it. No, people's been real nice to me. I never did get any razzing or anything. I've never had any problems, and I think one reason is I've always taken my turn. Nobody's ever made fun of me or anything that I ever knew of. I don't pick a fight, but I wasn't going to let nobody run over me. I could whip about anything that come around when I was in school.

Dinnertime. Chicken fry and potatoes in Kate's kitchen. Frozen apple pie and ice cream for dessert. Liz says it's the first time in weeks they haven't eaten dog. I blanch, and Liz adds that "dog" is bologna. Two hired men join us for the meal, and after coffee and cigarettes the afternoon's schedule is discussed. The men grow quiet as Kate gives out assignments with quiet authority. Liz will start disking a harvested wheat field for late-August planting. The hired men will take the combines out and finish cutting. Shirley will stay and wash up. Kate will mount a tractor and start spreading herbicide over the corn that's not being watered. Everyone except Shirley hops in pickups and heads out.

A lot of kids are raised on the farm, and they still don't like it. It just kinda depends on what you're like. I'm better satisfied here. I liked farm work from the start. I suppose a lot of it is the freedom you have. You get interested in watching this stuff grow, and it's fascinating. I think a lot of people would be just like me if they was ever out in the open and on their own. 'Course there's a lot of people got to have a boss, so there you are. Some people wouldn't do nothing if they didn't have a boss. But the freedom of farming gets in your blood. My dad had a heart attack on the tractor, and that was for him his retirement. I guess that will probably happen to me, too. I don't know what I'd do if I didn't work. There's no part of farming I dislike. There's a few jobs that you don't particular like, like picking up pipe when it's hot and things like that, but it all goes with it. (She pauses.) I've thought about quitting a few times, but I just kinda doubt if I could. Then again, most people's not an oddball like I am.

5 ❧ *Youth*

I was one of those people that wasn't good at sports. When I was a sophomore, we had this teacher who mentioned a bunch of writers like Voltaire and Hobbes and John Stuart Mill. Well, I took all these names down and went to the library to find out what these people had said. The library didn't have them. I remember the library didn't even have the *Odyssey* when I tried to read it. I spent a lot of time messing around with an erector set.

College student who left the county
and does not plan to return

THEMES OF YOUTH

To get popular in this school if you were a boy you would have to be good in sports. You would have to be good looking. You would have to be tuff.

Ninth Grader

Most of the girls that are popular have one thing in general. That is they use their best clothes for school. They dress their prettiest for school. Another thing that you have to do to be popular is smoke pot, drink. Have intercourse with boys . . . you can't be shy. You have to be bold and talk a lot. I'm happy to say I'm not popular. I never would want to be either.

Ninth Grader

To be popular you have to smoke pot, go to all the parties and act crazy.

Ninth Grader

Some girls are too much, like, I'm too good for you, or do you have a car? "Yes." Well, can I see how it feels? "Yes." So she gets in and this is not cool. Male & female relationship should come between each other 'cause they love each other. Not cause they feel like doing it. You got to have feeling in it. There is a difference in wham bam thank you mam, and making love. So when I date a girl, we go to the show, eat a hamburger or whatever she wants. Drive around & maybe kiss and that's it. Girls are not something to be played with, I mean treat 'em with respect, and they will like you. Once I was in love with a girl and we had a sex relationship. I didn't feel guilty. But also I had a sex relationship with a girl just to kill time, or maybe just horny. And I felt guilty. So you learn to have respect & treat 'em like they're someone.

Tenth Grader

I like small towns better than them huge cities. I guess why I like them so much is because I'm a country girl. I do a lot of rodeoing and so I wouldn't be much good any place else. In the small town there's always some country boy who are the best and one and only boy I could ever like.

Tenth Grader

I guess the reasons I like this town are normal reasons. 1. I've lived here since I was born which means I've lived here all most 17 years and this town is my home. 2. I like this town because my friends live here. Most of my classmates and I have gone to school together since kindergarten and it seems as if they are a part of me. 3. You know everybody that lives here in town and its nice to know people know you and can say "I remember when you were just so high."

But there are a couple of bad things to. 1) This town is little and the people here are so busy bodys. They know everything that goes on. 2) Also they judge people by the way they look. They don't give people a chance to try to let them know them. Maybe they are afraid they will like them or something. I don't really know for sure.

Some one can do something wrong! For example take drugs or something and people look at them for doing something wrong. They always look at the bad points in some one. Never the good points. 3) I just think I would

like to live in a bigger town where there's something going on.

Tenth Grader

Ten years from today, I will still be the same person I am today, but I will be physically different. The differences are as follows.

Mentally my thoughts will be older and wiser and probably more mature in thinking, but my character will be the same.

Physically my face will be older and more worn. My over all body will be larger and heavier. My legs and arms and the rest of my bodies muscles will be stronger and bigger. The hands will be tough and calisted but my hair will be much shorter.

Eleventh Grader

I like living in a small town because I don't feel alone in the world.

Twelfth Grader

Ivan Thomas: Nobody Will Touch You

Ivan Thomas struggles with the second-grade reader I have borrowed from the elementary school. He is stumped by the word "other," but recognizes the word that remains when I cover the "o" and the "r". On the third try he gets the correct pronunciation. He touches the cigarette pack in his shirt jacket but decides to wait. The next two sentences are clear sailing, but the word "danger" throws him off course again.

They told me that Special Ed was for kids that can't keep up with the other kids, or kids that are smarter than the other kids. Some places, they stick kids in there that got a higher I.Q. But nobody around here's got a higher I.Q. to be in there. Makes you think that it's for mentally retarded kids. One time, we went on a Special Ed trip, and we got to this school, and I asked one of the girls there where the bathroom was. And she asked me if I needed any help. Man, I about fell through the floor. If I needed any help! That's how people are. They think you can't do anything if you're in Special Ed.

It's pretty rough. Any time a new kid would move in, I'd be about the first one to meet him, and they'd hang around with me until they found out I was in Special Ed. Then they'd just turn: "Bugger off. Get lost." None of the girls'll talk to you or anything. I can go somewhere else and pick up a girl, just like that. I can take 'em out without everyone bugging me about it. Here, every time I ask a girl, guys will come over and try to steal her. They do that to me every time. I ain't the kind that's a brain, so I can't make up jokes. Then they won't go with me anymore, 'cause she met somebody that likes to joke around.

He comes to our house or the law office twice a week. I ask the librarian if she will read with Ivan the three days a week that the library is open. A retired first-grade teacher, the librarian is delighted to help. Ivan goes to the library twice and then never returns. He explains why: a girl he knows walked in and saw him hunched over a kid's book with the librarian. He can't risk being seen that way.

There's a lot of pot around here. There's nothing to do around here. It's not a honky community. Nobody likes to ride horses or anything like that, so they decided they'd be hippies, and they started smoking. About five or six kids really take hard drugs, shoot acid or pop pills. In the honky towns there's nothing to do, but the kids get drunk an' ride horses.

You can't do nothing unless you know how to read. Reading is the most important thing, really, in life. Knowing how to read. 'Cause if you can't read, you can't read a book or a newspaper. Find out what's going on. I was embarrassed pretty bad in biology. The teacher wanted me to read somethin', and I had to tell him that I didn't know how to read in front of everybody. In front of my best friend. He didn't know that I didn't know how to read. Boy, I's embarrassed.

I thought I'd quit school when I turned sixteen, but I decided not to. If you don't get out of high school with a high school degree, you can't find a job that's decent or anything. If I's to quit school, I wouldn't learn anymore, and I'm not too smart right now, so I really think I'll just stick it out. I'm thinkin' real hard about being a butcher. I worked at the grocery store in town, and I had a lot of fun cuttin' meat and everything down at the grocery store. I kinda think I'll go to butcher school. And I wanna learn how to read. Just nobody'd help me. I take arts and crafts, P.E., study hall. They just tell me I need it. I need all that junk.

Been going around in circles all my life. I wanna go somewhere where nobody knows me, so I can have friends and nobody won't know how it was here. Most everybody here knows your whole life story. What I really want to do is get out of Special Ed. Special Ed is like a prison. It surrounds you. It's like a disease. Nobody will go near you. Nobody will touch you.

Greg Daniels: Becoming a Fuller Person

It is spring break at the state university. Greg Daniels drives the 350 miles home with his two college roommates. All of them hail from the county. The day after he arrives, Greg comes to visit us and discusses his second year at college. He tells us that he's happy. He's also discovering that when you take the boy out of the county, you don't always take the county out of the boy.

I like the whole general atmosphere here. A lot of things I never really considered important or unique to this area mean a lot. Things that I just really grew up with. For instance, yesterday we were coming home and it was so clear. The sun was going down and there was a thin blue band over against the east. It was beautiful. At college one night, someone said, "Boy, isn't the sky clear tonight?" And I thought, "No, not really." It really wasn't. You could see some of the main stars, but that's about it. And the quiet. I think I miss that. Last night I got out of my car and turned it off and I couldn't hear anything. It's the first time I hadn't heard anything for months. (He laughs.) You know, there's things to see out here in the country that people don't realize. They think they have to go to the mountains to enjoy nature. I really like the mountains, but I miss not being able to see for miles and miles. You know, you can see the horizon thirty miles out here, and it's just perfectly flat.

Let's go back. Where did you grow up? How did you grow up? I've always lived in town. We were pretty close to the school and we'd play lots of football down by the grade school. Just all the things little kids do. We'd go out to Buffalo Point and hunt for arrowheads. Hang around the cliffs and roll rocks off. Play Cowboys and Indians. (He laughs.) The whole trip.

When I was about a fifth or sixth grader, I started working out on the farm. I didn't really work that hard out there the first few years. A lot of work is not, you know, sixth grader's work. Like moving thirty-foot joints of ten-inch irrigation pipe. So I'd end up driving the pickup back and forth.

By the time I was a freshman or sophomore, I was doing pretty well everything on the farm. You just have to concentrate on one job at a time and you pretty well get it down. You know how to plant. How to irrigate. How to work on engines.

I don't know. I've got a pretty good start on farming. A lot of basic knowledge. But to consider yourself a farmer, I think you'd almost have to make up your mind that you'd want to continue with farming. It seems to me that farming's kind of a state of mind as much as it is an occupation. I got awful tired of the dirt and the bugs and the heat.

Do you feel you were well prepared for college?

I've seen some kids that were more prepared in the knowledge of certain subjects. Physics. Calculus. But as a whole, I think I was prepared just about as well as anybody up there. To be able to relate to people. To problem-solve. To be happy and be satisfied with yourself as a person and as a student. I think I learned here about as well as I could've anyplace.

My mom really cultivated my interest in reading. When I was a little kid, she'd always get me to take a nap. She'd say, "Come on in and I'll read to you before your nap." I'd be asleep pretty fast, but I read quite a bit. I like novels. *Magic Mountain* is about my favorite book.

When I was getting ready to go to school, I wondered if people would look down on people out in the country as hicks or rednecks. But when I got to school, it seemed like it was just the opposite. It seems like a lot of people I've talked to almost look up to somebody who gets to stay outside and work with nature and go back to a small town and relate to just a small group of people really intimately like I do. They'd say, "What are you going to do this summer?" And I'd say, "I'm going to work on a farm." And they'd say, "Oh, really? You know, I'd really like to do that." So I didn't feel inferior at all.

What do you think you're going to do now?

I don't know. A college education is important to me more from the standpoint of becoming a fuller person than from the standpoint of learning how to do a job. I want to be financially secure, but I just don't want to grind through school and then start on a job. I don't know. I feel like some of the people at college, the professors and everything, have so much more in their life than I do and that I'd like to become more involved. I sometimes get the feeling that it'd be better if I just laid back for a couple of years and thought about things. Not stagnate, but just kind of think about everything. My life. What I want to do. What kind of job I want to get.

I really don't know. Me and my roommate are thinking about going to Nepal when we graduate. It's surprising how many friendships you can develop with people that come from such different places. And the more you discuss things with people, the more you realize what you've got in common.

A FEW FACTS ABOUT SCHOOL

It is just another high school day. In home economics, girls are embroidering seat cushions. In careers, boys are watching slides about the Air Force. In foods, students are making cin-

namon buns. In vocational agriculture, they are tearing down a tractor. In family living, they are diagraming football plays. In driver education, they are driving; in typing, they are typing; in shop, they are sanding; in mechanical drawing, they are throwing erasers; in band, they are drumming; in journalism, they are taking pictures of the gym. A few seniors who have elected senior English are doing crossword puzzles. The majority of juniors who have opted for business math over second-year algebra are adding columns of numbers on a balance sheet. In the office, in the teachers' room, in the gym, in this or that classroom, two or three upperclassmen each period putter around or sneak cigarettes while getting credit for teacher aid. At least one period a day, every student suits up and frolics in the gym. And every student every day partakes of corn dogs or hamburgers or chicken fry or chili in the school lunchroom.

According to Carol Oates, nothing has changed at the high school. And she ought to know. She graduated two years ago, but every weekend she drives 240 miles from college to home and makes a point of visiting with the kids up at the school.

In high school, if I didn't want to go, I didn't go. I'd never get in trouble for it. Whenever I had a job, I worked for my dad; and I came when I felt like it and left when I didn't. And I never went to camp. I don't think I'd been away from home for more than a week. I've gotten by all my life doing nothing. And I think that's kind of why I've done pretty bad in college. I should have been made to do things.

Twenty credits are required for high school graduation. Sixteen of the twenty must be "solid." The only subjects which are not "solid" are P.E., band, and teacher aid. Vocational-degree students must take two years each of English, mathe-

matics, social studies, science, and physical education. Academic-degree students must take, in addition, a third year of English. There are no course offerings in foreign languages or the fine arts; American history is the only history course.

I kind of felt I'd missed out a lot, not having art in school. I planned everything around art and I wanted it, but now I don't know if I'm qualified to do it or not. There's some really good ones in art, and then you feel like you don't have any business in that. I think the thing that really made an impression was when I'd go to shows and I couldn't appreciate the things that artists had made. And some people can really see stuff in art. I don't know. I think it would be good if they got more art because I was lost completely.

Up to half the senior class goes to college some years. "Going to college" is a phrase broad enough to include the rare occasion when a senior goes off to one of the four-year rural outposts of the state university system. More often it means (and is understood to mean) a two-year stint at the community college in the next county north, two or three years at an unaccredited Bible school to the south, or a year or two at barber, beauty, nursing, or automotive school. Community college is the favorite way station for students who don't marry or go into farming right after high school: they can enjoy the freedoms available in a rural town slightly larger than any to be found in the county while avoiding the traumas of diversified campus life; yet the school is close enough so they can drive home weekends to drag Main and pal around with old classmates. Serious female academics end up at the Bible colleges; serious male academics at the land-grant colleges, studying agricultural mechanics or ag-business. The elite—the one or two students each year with exceptional academic or athletic credentials—may try the main campus of the state university, more than 350 miles from home. They leave home with confidence, super jocks or brains who never have been seriously challenged; more often than not, they return home before the end of the first year. Painfully lonely, unschooled in meeting strangers, considered average when once they were considered special, they rejoice to be back in the "good ol' county."

We always used to talk about what we were going to do, and everybody I ever knew said one thing: "I'M NOT COMING BACK HERE AGAIN." And they'd go, but then they'd all come back. It's hard to get started knowing people, 'cause I've never done it. You always knew everybody. Unless a new family moved in. And that was a lot different than being the one that was doing the meeting. And I had never looked for a job before. You know everybody, and if you wanted a job, you could pretty well get it. I don't know. I think it's hard for some people here to leave, because they were really a big idol to a lot of people here, and now they're nothing. Or even if they were good in school, maybe straight As, you get to college, and you find out there's a lot of people like that too. It's kind of hard just to take off and leave.

Education may have been valued by the first pioneers who arrived from the settled East, but then education died. There were too many other problems associated with subsisting, surviving. It was as hard in the nineteenth century as it is now to entice teachers to stay; any female over sixteen and unmarried could tend the pot-bellied stove and stand over the neighborhood children with a stick. For the children of the newer arrivals, the first generation of natives, the East wasn't even a memory or a legend. The new West was generally slow to mature intellectually, and the county was one of its last extremities to feel any of maturity's stirrings. One did not think, one did not question to survive. One worked and prayed, maybe just worked. Education, least of all liberal education, never gained a foothold in county soil.

As the populace of the county tasted prosperity in the second half of the twentieth century, it has paid more attention to the schools. But athletics, not the three Rs, is the benefactor, perhaps because athletics ritualistically perpetuates the imagery of contest people know so well. All in all, it is fairer to say that liberal education in the county is a meaningless concept than to lament that the concept has been depreciated by the ages.

There's such a lack of something to do here. Something to keep people busy. You start driving when you're fourteen. Or thirteen. But I think the boredom is going to drive a lot of people crazy. Makes them do stuff they probably wouldn't have done, just out of complete boredom. Four girls were pregnant before they were married in my class. I did so many dumb things. I didn't even think. We used to drink when we partied, but a few kids started smoking. So I started doing that. I don't know what made me change. In the eighth grade, I was real big on sports. I was a cheerleader, and I never missed a game. And all of the sudden I was a freshman, and I wouldn't go to games if you paid me. I just felt they made too big a deal out of sports. A lot of my friends weren't in sports and used drugs and stuff. So other people would make remarks. Like in algebra, they was always saying, "She's probably stoned." One time they got a jock and put it in the mud and got it all dirty and put it in my locker with a poem.

For the seniors, the last baseball game, the last pep club cheer, signal an end to high school. The majority who by aptitude or determination were able to make the teams, male and female, will be prepared by high school to sit in the stands and cheer, to sit in the tractor cab or the cafe and grow a belly, to sit in the kitchen and spread. For a certain minority, however, high school was wounding. Lacking athletic prowess, a few have been shunted into oblivion all their high school days. They have suffered from the lack of art classes, language courses, facilities for golfing and swimming, and chess and theater clubs. Some become "road apples," their lives blooming only after dark; they get in trouble and drag Main toking or drinking. Others achieve good grades, acquire a mild appetite for knowledge, search in vain for Homer or nineteenth-century philosophers in the school and county library, and, finally, make peace with a life of loneliness and fantasy. If they do not heed the county's siren call before they have fully digested the novelties of time and change and diversity, they may turn the opportunity to attend a state college into permanent escape. The jocks, road apples, and cheerleaders stay until they die.

Bill Milligan: The Gamble You're Willing to Take

When I graduated from school, it was a matter of having to find a job. The practical thing of bringing in the money. Everybody talks about starting at the top, but I looked around and saw that teachers weren't being hired anyplace. I sent out at least three hundred applications all over the United States. I had my preferences, and I have my preferences now, but my goal was to be a teacher, and I needed a job someplace.

Monday afternoon. I am phoned to substitute the following day: several English classes, including the seniors, who are studying theater. To prepare, I walk over to the high school and visit the library. I cannot find an anthology of American theater.

I finally got a response here. I remember one day I got a long distance phone call, and they wanted me for an interview. I showed my wife the location on the map: a little dot in the middle of no place, a line through which is supposed to be a road. An ungodly, terrible place. But we decided we had to have a job, and we'd go to the depths of anything, no matter what it was going to be. I came down here, and the land kept looking worse and worse. I couldn't believe the land could get flatter, but it was still getting flatter and flatter and flatter. I finally got down here, and I thought, "There's no way I'm going to accept this job down here." But I was offered the job, and I signed a contract on the spot. Then the principal took me all around town to find a place for us to live. Some of the most terrible places you can imagine. I rented a house for eighty dollars. The day my wife came down here to move in, she took one look at that house and started crying. But, of course, we fixed the thing up, and it's livable now. You can almost see touches of grass in the lawn now.

The seniors file in. I am to show a film on the history of theater. A screen is unfurled. The film has no soundtrack, and I have the students take turns reading. I interject comments. The film traces the origins of modern tragedy and comedy. Vocabulary proves to be a major stumbling block. The students cannot pronounce many words, are unable to define subtle, pathos, rival, pantomime, anecdote, minstrel, tumult, corruption, secular. I make them look up words in the dictionary. More problems. They have never read a play or seen one; and they have never seen a mime. I attempt to supplement the

historical background. Fifth-century Greece. Someone asks, "What happened to it?" One student identifies Romeo and Juliet as dramatic figures. At the end of class, a boy comes up and asks where I come from.

Your reward in life is only as great as the gamble you're willing to take. This has been my philosophy for a long time. The other day, I was going through my pictures of last year's seniors. I went through them one by one. Married and living in town, married and living in town, married and living in town. And I came up with just a few of them that were still trying to make it outside of this town, independently. Now, there's nothing wrong with living in this town, and there's nothing wrong with getting married, but a lot of them don't realize that there is another world out there. They've never gotten to the point where they make a choice to stay. They're just so boxed in, they don't know there's an outside world. I don't know. Maybe they come back because they can't handle the situation away.

What causes this extreme homesickness? Kids talk an awful lot about wanting to be independent, but that's not what they really want. They want a coach or a teacher telling them what to do. They've never been away from home before, they've never seen the outside world. They have learned dependence on everybody else around here. They like security, and when they leave they can hardly wait to get back. They haven't learned to gamble.

I take my morning prep period in the teachers' room. Coach Johnson is at the little table in the center of the room playing solitaire. He has a formidable wad of snuff tucked behind his lower lip, and occasionally he expectorates into a coffee cup. There are two other teachers in the room: Andy Grout, the new English teacher, slumped in a frayed armchair, smoking Marlboros, popping Milk Duds, and grading a true-false test just administered to his tenth-grade English class; and Bill Milligan, the social studies teacher, sitting opposite Coach Johnson and preparing a current events test from Time *magazine for his seniors. In one corner of the room a senior girl hunts and pecks on an old upright typewriter; she's typing up the roster for tomorrow night's girls' volleyball game. Milligan asks Coach what Coach thinks about the senior boys' missing football practice. Coach works the snuff around a bit and plays the jack of diamonds to the queen. "Depends on when it is and the reason." He doesn't look up. Milligan hesitantly explains he wants to take a class social-studies field trip a week from Wednesday, to the state mental hospital to tour some of the wards. Coach continues to chew. "Bad time. Sub-district championships comin' up." From over in his armchair, Grout, who works with the defensive line, chimes in that Wednesday is always a critical practice day. Milligan doesn't press. He gathers up his magazine and his papers. "I guess I'll have to reschedule the trip." Coach grunts without looking up.*

Coaches have told me, "The only thing that makes this school great is sports." They say, "If it weren't for the football team, this school'd be nothing." Well, there's nothing wrong with being physically fit. It's good for the body, the mind, the attitude. But at the same time, I see an overemphasis. We've got our priorities changed around.

For example, there seems to be a prevalent attitude that we're giving too much homework—and shouldn't because of all the outside activities. So a lot of the teachers aren't assigning homework, because the parents and the administration say we've got too many activities. Yet the band is terrible, and there's no fine arts offered at all. A lot of the teachers say that if it wasn't for sports, so-and-so would drop out of school. That is probably true, but I still see a lot of other kids dropping out of school. What about these kids that can't excel in sports? We're not meeting their needs. Why can't something be done for them?

I would never raise a kid in this town. According to the team themselves, 85 per cent of them use drugs, and they're supposed to be the leaders. Possibly it's because there is a lack of things to do. That's what the kids say. In reality, there isn't so much a lack of things to do, but a lack of variety, cultural experiences. So every night you see kids dragging up and down Main Street, and this is the norm. Parents don't know if their kids are coming home for supper or where they're at. You always think of country people having a close-knit family structure, but we've found just the opposite. Every community has its drawbacks, but I see an awful lot of drawbacks in raising a kid right here. What happens if I have a skinny kid that can't excel in sports when sports is emphasized? I was always too small to make the teams; I would never have made it through this school.

Somedays you feel on top of the world. Today I feel like dropping out of teaching. Successes and failures. Until I got here, *Time* was an unheard-of kind of publication. The doctor read it and nobody else. My kids are required to read it, and sometimes they get excited about history, politics. This is a success. We like the people and are close to some, but we feel hemmed in by the system down here. Country people can be just as arrogant as city people. I don't see the dividing line between the two. I don't know. I'm used to greenery and the mountains. I guess I'm finding out that I really don't enjoy the flatlands.

6 ❧ *Belonging*

> Athletics has been something to me that gives me substance to hold on to. I loved sports. It was a way of being successful in something. It gave me the chance to be involved. To be associated. You know, I think most people want to be involved in something.
>
> *A county superintendent of schools*

FAMILIES

Some people like seventy-year-old Peewee Jackson have no family. They only have name. In the county, the Jackson name has always meant trouble.

One day after breakfast at the cafe, Peewee Jackson gets up from the liars' table and, instead of driving over to Main Street to sit in his pickup in front of the variety store, shuffles out into the cafe parking lot and drops dead. His brother Moon, the welder, takes up smoking again.

Now, none of the Jacksons have ever been churchy, and it's been fifty years since a county Baptist even said hello to someone with the Jackson name. So it looks for a time as if Peewee may not get a proper funeral in the town where he's spent his entire life. But proud Sam Wilson, the auctioneer, remembers the day when Peewee, if he was sober, could cowboy as well as any man around. And Sam just on principle doesn't like the idea of somebody born and raised in the county leaving it all alone. Sam makes sure the Methodist church will handle services and provides music himself. He and his wife sing "Beyond the Sunset" and "Heading for the Last Roundup." Before the pallbearers take the coffin out to the hearse, there is a covered-dish dinner in the Methodist church basement. After dinner, they take old Peewee out to the Pittsburgh cemetery in the country, north of where the old Pittsburgh town corporation thrived for ten years at the turn of the century. Peewee is buried thirty feet from the grave of the young preacher people say was gunned down in 1897 while trying to preach temperance in one of the cowboy saloons.

After the funeral, Sam Wilson goes to visit his mom, who is eighty. Mrs. Wilson spends her days taking care of her older sister, Minnie Sue, ninety, out on the ranch Minnie Sue wouldn't ever let them sell. Sam Wilson's mother has a milky complexion, an impish smile, fluffy white hair, and coal black eyes. She looks like a child's painting of a snowman. She remembers growing up in the county at the beginning of the century. As a school child, she once had to walk two miles from school in a bad snowstorm with a childhood chum named Wuntley. When they arrived at Wuntley's dugout, he became unbelievably formal. "Father," he called out. "I am come home." Old Mrs. Wilson has never gotten over that.

These days, she thinks of death. Sam was only thirteen when her husband died. Wilbur had just had a minor operation. He went out to gather cattle in the rain, came back wheezing, and died the next day. It was such a shock. Mrs. Wilson thought she'd never recover, but she did. She tells Sam to put her away if she ever gets "funny." She gets sick and has to go to the hospital. The nurse walks in when she wakes up and wants to clean her dentures. "Don't get excited," says the nurse. "I do it for folks all the time." Mrs. Wilson giggles. "You can't have my teeth," she says. "They're mine. They're still growing."

When she gets home, she writes a family history for the American Bicentennial. It ends like this: "My husband passed away in 1943. Sister Mildred was married to Arlis Glindell and for many years has made her home in California. She has two sons living near her. Only three of the original Arnold Dixon family remain; namely, Minnie Sue, Mildred, and myself, the writer of this article. We are fast turning things to our children and grandchildren, and to them we throw the torch. Please keep it burning."

At Thanksgiving, Christmas, and Easter, and sometimes in the fall after branding when lots of calf nuts can be pooled for a gigantic fry, families get together. It is never anything fancy. At Mrs. Green's, Thanksgiving at the old homeplace out in the country means forty-five cars and pickups in the driveway, swarms of children at play from the grape arbor to the hog-farrowing houses. It means that every female locked into the family's breast by blood or marriage brings a contribution to the five massive tables set up in the kitchen, in the dining room, and on the sun porch. Grandma Green, of course, is in full command. She supervises the proper categorical arrangement of the dishes: the fruit pies, cakes, jellos, and custards to the sun porch; the turkeys, the one overcooked roast (out of deference to Al the Cowman, Mrs. Green's oldest), the cornbread stuffing, the bread stuffing, the rice stuffing, the noodles, and gravy to the dining room; the pork and beans, green beans, and broccoli, the biscuits and homemade bread, the boiled, fried, and creamed potatoes, the five cranberry concoctions, and the seven salads to the living room.

Before dinner, Grandma and her daughters and daughters-in-law busy themselves in the kitchen, mixing up iced tea, warming the biscuits and bread, and slicing the turkeys. The granddaughters oversee the mischief of their toddlers and ambulatory young, while the adult males of the second and third generation stand about in the grassless yard trading observations about the frost, the cattle market, the auctions; some of the younger third-generation males stand about in their own little corner of the yard comparing their new Stetsons and Sunday boots and flowered shirts. Fourth-generation youngsters buzz in and about the adults, gracelessly scooping up endearments and indulgences from uncles, great-uncles, aunts, and older cousins of both sexes.

During and after the meal, homage is paid to the present. In the dusty living room, whose furnishings Grandma hasn't altered in five decades, new offspring are handed about and scrutinized for physical vestiges of Great Granddad's eyes and Great Grandma's delicate fingers. Beneath the pictorial history of the family lining the walls in delicate wooden picture frames, the aging of the elderly is discussed along with the developing loyalty of those in other rooms who have recently entered the family by marriage. There are casual financial reports and predictions among the men and, in the women's circles, comparisons of children, recipes, diets, and household acquisitions. This is the present.

But as the afternoon wears on, conversation shifts to the past. Suddenly the days when the dead were alive return, the days when the old were young and the young unborn.

Grandma gets out the scrapbooks from the old wood dresser in the attic. Crumbling brown paper sacks full of letters and postcards and buttons and decaying yellow photographs are emptied onto the living room floor. Stories of character and strength and hardship and foolery are told and retold for the hundredth time. There is exquisite lingering pleasure as the old memories become familiar again. Grandma dominates, but occasionally Grandpa or one of the older children contributes. Uncle Wilbur was a visiting type. See your wagon dust a mile away and get out there in front of the house to flag you down, always make you stay for dinner, supper if he could. Old Reuben, never forget the day he moved Aunt Mary's outhouse on Halloween night and then came back by later, maybe had a pint of whiskey in him, and fell right in the hole himself. Great Grandma Millstone could pick a good steer better'n her old man. Just had that kinda knack. Never went wrong. Now, Al, that's where you got the charm yourself.

The boys, Mrs. Green's children, remember their own memories: about the time Al and the other older ones threw fresh cow dung on baby Junior's first cowboy hat out at the barn; about going to town in the wagon and watching Granddad break mean horses down at the corral; about the broomcorn johnnies bedded in the well house who stole Al's underpants off the clothesline when he was twelve; and about how Al retaliated by stealing their poker pot when they were drunk and refused to give it back until they turned over his underwear. The third- and fourth-generation children sit in rapt stillness, nodding with wonder and amusement as the stories are embellished, nodding with practiced sobriety when Grandma adds a biblical or commonsensical moral to every tale. There are no surprises. The stories have been told many times before, will be told many times again. But the repetition is satisfying.

At dusk the women go back to the kitchen to make more iced tea, to reheat the biscuits and breads, and to tidy and rearrange the laden tables so everyone can eat again. This time, the repast is called supper. The toddlers are sleeping, and some of the oldest fight the urge to sleep. When darkness falls, the family begins to disperse. Farewells are short and casual, sometimes neglected completely. Christmas is coming.

Doc Pete: And the Honorable Have Dishonor

If I'm in a big city and I have a coronary, I'm not missed. If I'm killed, I'm not missed. But I want to be a person that counts, so I came here.

For thirteen years, he was a Baptist missionary in Africa. He returned to the States to be able to make enough money to put his children through college and chose the town from a number of practice locations suggested by the mission group. "I knew when I came here that there was a sort of independent-minded people here. I think they are as human as David was, because David was called a man after God's own heart, and yet we know that he had some very earthy parts about him." His oldest son, Jim, went on to medical school and now has returned to practice with his father. Doc Pete and Doc Jim work out of a clinic attached to the town hospital. Doc Jim now carries the load in obstetrics, Doc Pete in geriatrics; neither one is frequently seen outside the clinic, the hospital, or church.

You can do what you want to here. We're a little like Robinson Crusoe. I can do a caesarian section. I can do a hysterectomy, a gall bladder operation. I do psychiatric work, family counseling. Internal medicine, skin work, plastic surgery, bone and joint work. There is one thing, and that is that you're all things to all men. Anyway, that's what we are out here. You're the intern, the resident, the visiting man, the orderly. If you want a man catheterized, you catheterize him. You don't order him to be catheterized. And this saps your strength. You pay for it. But I enjoy the work. I don't enjoy affluence, but I enjoy a lot of work. I wouldn't be surprised if the people around here enjoy their work too. They have a lot of stuff in 'em. I don't really know what keeps them here. It may be what keeps me here. It just may be that we're the same breed of cat. You know? I've been here thirteen years, and I feel sort of liberated in a way.

How's that?

I actually have some problems. I have fairly deep guilt feelings when I get things that are too easy. I can't see it outside, away from here. I don't know what it's like in the city anymore. But I can't imagine a thirty-hour week. I just can't imagine. I do that almost in one day. I mean it. (He chuckles.) I don't suppose I'm typical for the profession. In fact, I'm not even typical for the county medical society. I can't communicate with my colleagues. I don't even try. I do preach, but I don't try to make comrades out of my colleagues. I've never brought litigation, for example, to collect a debt. Never. A lot of people just don't have the money. And I'm not about to take a pickup away from a farmer when that's the last thing he has. I know that the doctors around here charge ten dollars for an office call. We charge six dollars. It was years ago that I passed the

$100,000 mark in my write-offs. On my accounts receivable written off. I could have retired on that much money. But it really wasn't worth collecting. As far as I'm concerned, all there would be is grief.

The people have come. We gather people from 150 miles away. It's sort of like having a pen pal. You just develop an interest in one another. I often think that being a physician is like being married. You don't feel that your wife is Miss America, but she's the one that you want to confide in. But you have to be pretty good, on top of things. If you wouldn't want to be a quarterback, you wouldn't want to be a doctor here. I think that you're throttled up when you try to deliver services in the city. You can't use the extent of your capabilities and your training. When you're out in a place like this, where you're the authority, and you're sort of the last one they come to, and the only one, you can use everything you've got. I feel it's less the problem of delivering health care in a rural area; it's the problem of not having amenities. Your wife has to be amenable to this, because there is no high society. If you want to go hear a concert or something, it's two hundred miles one way.

What do people die of here?

People die of heart attacks. Cancer. Old age. And we have a high level of injury from farm accidents. Like, for instance, I had a rush situation just about ten miles east of here. Will Schmidt got his foot caught in a grain auger. It was pretty badly mangled. I had to reach down there in the grain with my pocketknife and amputate his leg. He's a Christian. He just sat there in that dumb ambulance saying, "Praise the Lord." (He chuckles.) You know, these are things that make you feel you're really needed. These men take upon themselves all sorts of fantastic types of work, and they do very dangerous things on the farm. In this instance, I had ten minutes from the time I heard about it till the time I had to amputate. You feel you have to make your decisions. You're needed when you have to do that. It thrills you when you have the opportunity to work that way.

I treat people who came out here in covered wagons. They grew up in dugouts. They're current patients. Things like that add vigor and vitality to a practice. I handle most of the older people. It has just really been a hard thing for me, because it makes me see what I'll be fifteen years from now. And I just don't want to get old. (He laughs.) Even before my son came back, I almost didn't make it. I was being pushed. I got so the nurses had to write down my orders for me. I couldn't write. I couldn't sign my name. I didn't know my son would come back here to practice until a month before he came. It's really great. It's sort of like being raised from the dead, really.

There's a group of people here at the end of the road. Do you know what a burned-out outlaw is? Somebody that doesn't feel like fighting it anymore. I mean, they don't want to rob a bank, they don't want to kill anybody else, but they don't want to answer for what they've done. They come here. These fellows at the end of the road do come here. They work on the farms. They live honorable lives. They often marry, have children. They lose their former identity. And we treat them. We also treat a lot of wetbacks. Very easily. We don't interfere at all. We don't report anything. We're doctors. We're not working for the border patrol.

There's a lot of alcoholism. They use it for medical purposes. Too often. They're too proud to come to a physician. So they treat their problems with alcohol. Can't sleep or marital difficulties or psychiatric problems. You just have to be patient and kind. I sober them up, and I don't preach to them, because they've had enough sermons. But you know, one thing bothers me about alcohol. I don't know why everybody's not an alcoholic. Just to tell you the truth, I don't think the talented individual has the wherewithal to turn himself off. And then he turns to alcohol. One of the beautiful things about my work is that I have tranquilizers to use. And mood elevators. They're the ones that take people out of a depression. Boy, it sure is nice to be able to help people out when they're depressed. As far as I'm concerned, every household in the United States should have something in the medicine cabinet bordering on a narcotic for pain and something that will put you to sleep, a tranquilizer. I think everybody should have a tranquilizer on hand. Everybody has a potential drug problem, don't we?

For all their loveliness, the people around here don't deal in thought. That's hard for me. And I haven't told you about the blemishes. For instance, a fellow came in and asked me if there was anything he could give his wife because he'd been having intercourse with the cattle. There's just no way to file that down into your deepest soul and say it's beauty. But it is true: these things happen. And the honorable have their dishonor.

Part of devotion is demanded by austerity. The best is brought out in people by trial. My blessings have never been things that have done me a favor. It's just always been my trials. Adversity has been my friend and teacher. But I get awfully discouraged. I get terribly despondent. I work hard, and there are lots of things that don't come out well, I have to leave behind. I always have my back to the things that are good, and my face to the things that are still needing care. And that is disappointing. I'm always seeing people that still have a death yet to happen in their lives.

TEAMS

The homecoming parade turns down Main Street a little after two on the Friday afternoon before the game. By then, the street is cleared of cars and jammed with parents and school kids. At the head of the procession, the police chief creeps along at two miles an hour, blinking his Mars light and looking more self-important than usual. Behind the chief comes the parade, that peculiarly random assemblage of vehicles, beasts, and humanity that always makes parades in the county seem almost accidental. The mounted flag detail clomps right along at the police chief's bumper, followed by a squad of thirty junior high school boys on bicycles and motorbikes, old cars driven by old farmers, skimpy floats on flatbeds, the baby-blue First Baptist Church school bus, the band, the homecoming queen candidates on the hoods of their parents' passenger cars, new tractors and combines from the dealerships, a mounted brigade of horses and riders specially formed for the parade and, at the very rear, the big cement truck of the new sand-and-gravel outfit in town.

And then, suddenly, there is nothing. No more. The parade has come and gone. All three and a half minutes of it. The flurry has come and gone. The pomp and excitement and school pride have come and gone. There will be nothing more in the way of parades until the county fair next August. But for reasons known to those who have never seen anything better, there is no grumbling. Small children are enraptured; the adults and teens are satisfied. Only Abe Berkowitz gibes, but that's Abe. Been here thirty years and still puts on the dog. Nobody else would think of poking fun. Wasn't a great parade, but wasn't all that bad either. Better than last year, in fact. And tonight, after dark, there will be a good game, the never-too-often-tasted sweetness of victory.

Red-faced, the new superintendent hesitantly tells the new school board what happened. The school board members keep straight faces, as if concerned, as if these things didn't happen every year. . . .

In the gymnasium locker room the new lettermen are blindfolded. Shoes and socks removed. Someone has already "taken a bowel movement in the stool" to create the "odor of feces." Eggs are broken on the cement floor around the stool. The initiates are told to walk carefully to avoid stepping in the squishy matter they are advised is "feces." They climb on chairs, blindfolds still in place, and jump off with whole raw eggs in their mouths; they bob for apples in tubs of vinegar; they reach blindfolded into the toilet bowl to retrieve bananas they are told are not bananas; they strip and pick marshmallows up off the floor with their cheeks; the act completed, they eat marshmallows identified as the ones they have picked up. It goes on and on. Blindfolds are removed. For the weenie race, frankfurters are secured in hindquarters. The initiates race around the gym, striving not to drop the impediments. Frankfurters break off; boys are sent to the restroom to "strain." It goes on. Naked, the boys are plastered with molasses and feathers. They race up and down Main Street in the cool autumn evening. It goes on. The next day at school, the new lettermen wear wooden school letters around their necks. Pencils with strings attached are dangling out of their shirt fronts. All day, they must ask girl students to sign their letters. The girls use the pencils hanging out of the initiates' shirt fronts. At the other end, each pencil has been securely fastened by string to the initiates' "privates."

Although its student body rarely exceeds 130, the high school produces championship teams year after year. The town appreciates this. The boosters raise money to videotape the games, the coaches work long hours, and when the boys play basketball, be it at home or a hundred miles away, more townfolk turn out for the game than for the county fair. Snazzy in their white-and-fuchsia uniforms with their names on the backs, the boys run intricate drills during the halftime break of the less-exciting, but not less-supported, girls' game. The fans go wild. The band bleats dissonant percussion, the cheerleaders kick and leap.

> All for the Buffs stand up! (clap, clap)
> All for the Buffs stand up! (clap, clap)
> We won't shut up till y'all stand up
> So all for the Buffs stand up! (clap, clap)

When the boys take the floor for their own game, the town supporters stand and clap in rhythm while the team snakes through the rest of its complicated drills—layups, passes, jumpers. As the announcer booms out the names

of the starting players over the P.A., the young men sprint to the center of the floor to be recognized, slapping their teammates' palms. The hometown crowd's cheering drowns out the announcement of the names, but nobody needs to hear them anyway. They know their boys. From tipoff to final buzzer, the gymnasium rocks with the band's fanfares and the fans' clapping and booing and screaming, in response to which the boys exhibit their style of scrappy, hustling aggressiveness, time after time overcoming opponents much better than they by dint of sheer spunk, a Boston Celtics fastbreak offense combined with a full-court zone press patterned after the championship teams John Wooden coached at UCLA. It is exciting, winning ball-playing. It is something to be proud of. The kids out on the floor are your kids. You played on and cheered for the same team in high school, and you played against the parents of the kids who are playing your kids; and when there's not much to be proud of in this sorry old blowing country, goddamit, the kids put up a real good fight. . . .

GOING TO STATE

After the girls take district in volleyball, the town begins to gear up for State. The county paper fills with supportive ads by local merchants. Photos of the team players are posted on store fronts up and down Main Street. School is officially canceled for the tournament days, and the purple-and-white school bus is marshaled to carry supporters up to the state capital. Car pools are organized, and the town empties the day before the tournament begins. I travel to Denver with Denise Wright. Two other Wright girls (cousins) are on the team.

Wednesday night we synchronize watches and agree to leave at six the next morning. I am up and ready before it is light. At nine, Denise hasn't shown, so I drive over to her trailer. Pandemonium. Dishes are piled up, clothes are scattered about. Denise has left her two-year-old with a babysitter and chased around the fields to give her husband a second good-bye kiss; now she's hunting for a house key. She drinks a can of pop and cleans up a package of M&Ms for a chaser. Finally she finds the key, puts the last satchel in the car. We drive by her mother's to leave the key and then head for the highway. Ten miles up the road, Denise discovers she's forgotten her purse. Back to her mother's for the key, back to the trailer, back to her mother's, back on the road again. It is close to noon as we drive past the liquor store west of town. Denise tells me she read that favorite colors are a clue to personality. Unfortunately, she doesn't have a favorite; she likes them all. This is supposed to be a sign of a personality not yet fully formed.

I got married when I was sixteen. It was April of my sophomore year. I finished out that year, but I never did go back to school. I don't know. I guess I thought I was bigger, and they couldn't tell me what to do since I was married. But a girl still really needs her mama when she's sixteen. Heck, I was just a little kid. Now, I keep thinkin' I don't even think I probably loved him. I don't think I coulda knowed. I went crazy over him. See, Stan is four or five years older than me, and when I started dating Stan, we didn't just drag Main. He took me to different towns, and we ate supper, and we went to drive-ins in Kansas. He brought me things, things like that. None of the other boys were old enough to drive around like that. I just thought he was it.

Denise spends most of the next six hours talking. She talks about fights she's had with various girls in town and how she once wound up in a hair-pulling match on Main Street. She identifies the parties to various illegitimate pregnancies, which she assures me is not gossip since everyone knows all of it anyway. She tells me about the time she was thrown off a horse and how she almost lost her baby when a cow kicked her in the stomach. She describes how people with brown and blue preferences can build empires together. She comments on high school dating, drugs, the drinking scene. I hear about marital spats she and Stan have had over the years and the times she has made him beg her for forgiveness. She laughs at her naiveté and recalls the first time she saw a calf being pulled out with a winch and chain. Stan told her the cow had swallowed a log chain, that they were pulling the chain out of her rear end. For weeks she goes around telling everyone about the poor cow who swallowed the chain.

We stop at a Pizza Hut off the highway for a late lunch. Denise borrows a pen, turns her placemat over, and completes a word scramble. Another mat has a map of the thirteen colonies, and since I'm from New York, Denise thinks I ought to fill in the states. I do. We eat thick, chewy pizza and guzzle Cokes. Denise buys two candy bars for the road. Soon we're on our way again. A cattle truck lumbering past us in the opposite direction reminds Denise her father might be in the vicinity. She switches on the CB. Her dad's handle is Casey Jones. Hers is Calamity Jane. Soon she learns her father is loading cattle twenty miles away. She leaves a message with a trucker (Wild Man) to tell Casey Jones that Calamity Jane is on her way to State. She leaves the CB on for a while. To me it is mostly static, a few comprehensible words of English. "Looks pretty good in that T-Bird," a Safeway trucker remarks. Denise enjoys the compliment. Someone wants her number. Someone warns of police action a few miles up the road. De-

nise tires of the exchanges. She switches off the CB and inserts a cassette in the tape deck, sets the cruise control at sixty, and leans back and relaxes.

When you're married, things change. Your girlfriends at school aren't even the same. There you have a house to take care of and clothes to wash and dry, and there they are, still out having a good time. At sixteen, you don't think about cookin' and cleanin' and those things. All I thought was, "Well, my God, I can see him every day and every night." But some of the fits I used to throw! If I'd cook something, and he wouldn't say how scrumptuous it was, well, I'd get mad and bawl. I'd always tell him, "I hate you, I want a divorce." One time, we got in a fight, and the next morning I was still mad, and I got up and packed all my clothes up, and me and my girlfriend, we went and stayed all night in a motel. (She laughs.) That's just because I didn't have no business being married when I was that young. Now I look upon it, and those fights don't mean nothin'.

We are on the outskirts of Denver. The evening rush hour has begun, and the frenzy of car lights is alarming even to me after the miles of empty horizons. "Do all these people know where they're going?" Denise cannot imagine that they do. Neighboring automobiles and their drivers are a source of great interest. Houses along the expressways are also interesting, especially two-story structures. "I bet you that two-story has a basement." I navigate as she drives. We reach the Howard Johnson's where the team is being housed. In the lobby we encounter half the population of the town.

Our room is 517. The elevator ride is the climax of the trip. Denise feels as though her stomach will fall out. "Is this it?"

she asks when the elevator stops and another passenger gets out. I point to the lighted numbers on the panel and restrain her from a premature exit. We deposit our stuff in the room. Denise inspects the amenities: color television, bed lights, telephone, temperature control. We go downstairs and check out the restaurant, the sauna, the swimming pool; then back upstairs with Howard Johnson sandwiches. Denise turns on television and announces she has to wash her hair. It is waist-length, blond, and western-styled. After she finishes showering, she sits on a bed and tucks the long strands around rollers. She's brought her drier along, and for the next two hours she sits in bed and watches television to the hum of the drier. I learn she does her hair five times a week at home. Stan fortunately finds the sound of the drier motor soporific.

I'm glad we had the baby when we did, because I was getting bored. There's nothing to do if you don't have a job when you're married, and there's nothing to housekeeping until you have kids. I growed up a lot, and it made us stronger, 'cause Stan's a good father, and I look at Stan a different way now. He was the one that was wanting to have a baby more than I was. The baby's two, so I would only have been eighteen. None of my girlfriends had kids, so I wasn't really wanting one; but when I did get pregnant, I was babied, and everybody made a big deal out of it. (She laughs.) I loved that baby with all my heart. I'd sit all day and hold him. He was so sweet, and I just couldn't believe it. It's a miracle, miracle, miracle, that he could come from Stan and I's love. I would hold him when he was asleep. I never laid him down. Everybody used to get onto me, especially my mother. She said, "Denise, don't set and hold that kid when he's sleepin', let him lay down so he'll rest better." And it probably woulda been right, but I just didn't. It was just me and Cody all day long.

Morning. Primping before the mirror, breakfast, shopping. Denise wants to know if I played bingo when I lived in the city. She's heard that you can win good prizes. She decides she'd like to find a Montgomery Ward store because she's ordered a pair of pants through the catalog and now she'd like to find the jacket. We check the sale racks at Wards and browse in various shops on a mall. Denise sprints across the floor at a discount house and takes advantage of a two-minute sale to buy a purse. Soon it's mid-afternoon, time to head for the gymnasium where the state tournament is beginning.

We sit with the town contingent behind a purple-and-white banner, close to two hundred of us in the bleachers. The opposition sits across from us, and they've brought along a band that plays spirited fight songs, but our rhythmic clapping almost rivals the trombones and drums. The girls on the team emerge from the basement locker room, suited up in fuchsia and white. They slap hands and huddle with the coach. The referees whistle the game into play. We stand and applaud: fast, rhythmic clapping. The match will be the best two out of three. There is much individual exhortation. "Heads up, girls!" "Watch that ball!" "Come on, Marilyn!" "Oh, no, Suzie!" Ola fumbles. So does Marilyn. The crowd screams and the coach replaces Ola, but her replacement fumbles too. Ola returns to the game. Very quickly, the other team is ahead. We make a recovery of sorts, but it comes too late. We lose the first game by a wide margin. The mood is tense, but then someone begins to clap and soon we're all burying our anxiety in team cheers.

Game two goes well. The opposition is bigger and more

proficient, but our girls are quick. We establish an early lead. The coach calls for time out. The audience roars encouragement, and everyone stands for the girls. The team runs back on the court. We maintain our lead, but the opposition is catching up. Marilyn delivers some good serves; Ola hammers in some good spikes. Carol steps over the line when she serves, and we lose the ball. The crowd is incensed: "Watch that line!" But the error is not fatal. The score is tied on several occasions. The girls crouch on the court awaiting each serve. The score is 14–12, our favor. Last point . . . maybe. Denise squeezes my knee, and we all stand up for this one. The chanting is deafening. "ONE MORE POINT, ONE MORE POINT!" My mind races to 1972, Miami: FOUR MORE YEARS, FOUR MORE YEARS! But there is little time for rumination. Marilyn does it. The game is won. The crowd is ebullient, jumping and shouting. Denise hugs me, I hug Denise, we each hug ten other townspeople. We're back in the game.

Game three begins with a wicked serve from the opposition. Another one follows. Our girls are losing confidence. A ball lands in the center of our court, and no one moves to volley it. Another ball is spiked into the hole where one of our girls is out of position. The other side takes to booing when we score, so we boo in retaliation. As the score worsens, there are angry shouts from the fans. Finally, there is despair, silence. We lose the game badly. We lose the match. Some parents have tears in their eyes, and everyone is glum. The victory celebration at a Mexican restaurant will have to be canceled, and everyone will return to the gym for the girls' evening consolation match. Something may be salvaged there, but the plum is gone. We won't be state champs this year.

I would never let my daughter get married at sixteen. There are just so many things I missed. I love Stan, but I wish I could've met him about maybe six years later. I just never really got to do a lot of things I would have loved to have done. I'm so scared of big cities and things like that, and I always wanted to go to college and have a roommate. Just to see what it's like, because I think that's something I'll always think about. I didn't really finish my education at all. I don't know. It makes you wonder if you would've went on, what your life could've been different in.

7 *Saturday Night, Sunday Morning*

To be converted, to be regenerated, to receive grace, to experience religion, to gain an assurance, are so many phrases which denote the process, gradual or sudden, by which a self hitherto divided, and consciously wrong, inferior and unhappy, becomes unified and consciously right, superior and happy, in consequence of its firmer hold upon religious realities.

WILLIAM JAMES, *The Varieties of Religious Experience*

NIGHTSONGS

The nighttime sounds of the open plain echo all the way to the town.

On the cold January night when Whimp Billings' hoist broke and he was pinned beneath a stock tank, Millard Williams heard his cries for help. Millard was in town, three miles away, lying awake in his bed at 2:00 A.M. and counting the dollars he was going to lose that day when he finally sold the fat steers he'd been feeding out at Al the Cowman's feedlot.

Al the Cowman's feedlot is almost two miles from town. For several weeks in the late fall, when he takes his range calves off their mothers and locks them in pens at the feedlot for weaning, the bawling of the calves drowns out the 8:00 P.M. tolling of "A Mighty Fortress Is Our God" from the bell tower of the town's Methodist church.

In the summer, the deep, open-throttled rumbling of irrigation pump engines floods the prairie. The only other sound in July and August is the noise the corn makes as it grows. In the fall, the harvesters sometimes work through the night till dawn, and the people in town sleep to the rhythm of their machines: the dull roar of the combines straining above the metallic churning of the corn and milo headers, and the high-pitched whine of the grain driers at the elevators, humming around the clock for months, not resting until the last hopper load of corn has been moisture-cured and stored in November or December.

During planting and harvest, night passes quickly, so it merges quickly with day. During the dead of winter, the thunderous stillness on the prairie at night weighs heavily on the soul, sometimes producing desperation, more often compressing lives into flat concentrations of safe routine. Television is the mainstay of routine.

Apart from television, night routine expresses itself according to the variables of age, temperament, and public-spiritedness. For the teenagers there are school activities and 4-H and the old standby of dragging Main. For civic-minded adults there are council meetings, school board meetings, Booster Club meetings, lodge meetings, sorority meetings, and salad suppers. For the saved there are Wednesday-night prayer meetings, and for the not-saved there is Wednesday-night poker. Ball games are universal succour against the oppressiveness of night.

A cold January evening at an abandoned schoolhouse. On Tuesday nights it becomes the Odd Fellows' lodge. Men stand around visiting. I am introduced. The Past Grand says it's time to begin, so the men don long velvet robes (but not long enough to conceal pointed toes of cowboy boots), and I am conducted to an adjoining pantry, left alone behind a locked door. I can hear the cadence of cowboy boots marking out ritual marches in the hall, the tattoo of the Vice Grand's staff on the wooden floor, muffled voices chanting in unison. A robed marshal comes to the pantry. I am blindfolded. Secret rap on the door, secret password whispered into the wicket. The marshal guides me blindfolded into the hall and from station to station. Familiar voices, stumbling over polysyllabic words from the ritual book, instruct me in the mysteries and wisdom of Odd Fellowship. The blindfold is removed. Noble Grand instructs in hand signals and passwords and administers the penultimate oath. Chanting: I AM AN ODD FELLOW! I AM AN ODD FELLOW! Corn bread and beans for refreshments.

The county's night life is a world of moral ambivalence, celebrated by plaintive female voices telling of angels and fallen women, good-woman men and rakehells, hard work and the bottle, Christian charity and nonsupport. Three or four times a year, the song of the county's moral ambivalence becomes nightsong itself, and willy-nilly routine and desperation dissolve beneath its enchanting strain.

The pretext for nightsong varies, but the medium is always dance: on New Year's Eve, the dance sponsored by the Odd Fellows, at the abandoned stone school gymnasium fifteen miles north and five west of town; in June, the dance at the elementary school gym, following the annual high school alumni reunion banquet at the town's community center; in late August, the dance at the county seat that climaxes the county fair. At these dances, there is never a bar, but everyone gets drunk. There is no lewdness, but everyone gets kissed. There is no shame, but three generations of families make fools of themselves in front of each other.

People come from miles around, from other counties and other states, the nightsong of the county is so well known. Gym floors are strewn with sawdust, lights are dimmed, balloons and streamers are hung from the ceilings. Cowboy dress is required. The young studs wear tall black Stetsons, ornate tooled leather belts with their names blocked on the back, extra-tight blue jeans, bright western shirts, and shined-up boots, while their women come in even tighter jeans with pullovers just as tight, name belts, and the same pointy-toed boots. Among the older set, the men prefer colored Levi boot-cuts and go hatless; the older women stick with the basic Sears pantsuit and sandal combination.

People dance the jitterbug and the western stomp and the western polka to the fast tunes, the two-step and the basic crotch-walk to the slow tunes. In the crotch-walk, the female wraps her legs around the male's right leg and rides his knee as he jerks around the floor in time to the music. But the special feature of nightsong festivity is "intermish," which goes on in the parking lot. Grandmas, grandpas, moms, dads, sons, daughters, and other kin gather around cars and pickups to drink and socialize. The standard libation is swamp water, sometimes called river water and said to contain pollywogs. The vehicles around which the swamp water is imbibed are known as watering holes. Swamp water may be grapefruit juice laced with grain alcohol in a five-gallon milk jug, or Coke and Heaven Hill in a plastic thermos. At the June alumni dance and the August fairtime dance, the watering holes are circles of giggling good spirits at the lowered tailgates of pickups. On New Year's Eve, they are crushed bodies stuffed into passenger cars with motors running and heaters blasting. The swamp water never runs out. When one watering hole dries up, intermishers move on to another, and even out-of-staters mix roles as hosts and hosted.

Dancing becomes more intimate, intermishes more frequent as the evening wears on. Men and women give rodeo whoops of excitement. By midnight, young couples are grinding and clinching shamelessly, and the crotch-walkers have slowed to a simple humping rhythm. Women plaster wet kisses on their best friends' husbands. The oldsters waltz with teetering grace and dignity around the outside of the floor, stopping now and again to trade partners, embrace children and old friends. Sons and grandfathers drunkenly hug each other and giggle; and proud, happy daughters nimbly lead their glaze-eyed fathers through slow, romantic two-step numbers. Shy farmers and cowboys, braced with swamp water, expound volubly on love and friendship and passion, surprising their neighbors with a greater repertoire of English words than has been heard all through wheat, corn, and calving.

And then at two or three in the morning nightsong, like a good rain, vanishes into the black heavens as quickly as it came. The next morning, the hay has to be mowed, the cows fed, and the crops watered. The stolid prairie folk slip back into their modest little prairie homes.

Janet Lou Martin: Awful Big Companies for Me to Take Care of My Song

I'm just a nobody that wrote a song that hit. It was the chance of a lifetime. And then I come up against someone with the big companies that stole it.

She lowers the record player arm, and the diamond makes contact with the plastic. Static. "Listen now, Jessie." The sound is Nashville, the lyrics country. Maybe I've heard it before, maybe I haven't. When the arm lifts, I voice admiration and praise. Janet Lou tenses and begins to talk. Sometimes there's a cold glint in her eyes.

On November 27, we were coming home from Amarillo, Texas, and it was on Thanksgiving Day in 1969, and Bill was settin' there and drivin'. We went down to see Merle Haggard. Bill was tired and sleepy and rather bored, and I was trying to think of something funny to say. So I looked at him and I said, "Guess I'll write a song about Daddy was a preacher, Mama was a barroom girl." And he looked at me kinda funny. And then I said, "Daddy was a preacher, Mama was a go-go girl." He laughed, and he said, "Well, it might be all right." I had a little piece of paper, and I started writing. And by the time I got home, I had quite a bit of it down. And I turned the tape recorder on, and I kept writing until I come out with pretty near what I wanted.

I wasn't for sure what the public would think of something like that. I didn't know how people would like me to mix a preacher with a go-go girl. So then I called a publisher I knew in Amarillo, and I was talking to him, and at first he wasn't too excited about it, but the more he got to thinking about it, why he was. So in two days I registered it through the mail. I usually type the words out and put it on tape, and I wrap it and tape it real good, go to the post office, and they stamp it real good, and I register it back to myself. Never open it up. It was copyrighted in December 18, 1969.

Then my publisher decided we should go to Nashville and record it. He said he found a girl in Amarillo that could sing this song. But she couldn't sing it unless I was singing it with her, and she hadn't learned it quite well enough by the time we was ready to go. So my publisher said, "Why don't you go ahead and sing it?" I said, "Well, you know, I hadn't planned on it." And I come home laughing about that. But I got to considering it, and in two weeks of that time I was back there. But on my way to Nashville it really dawned on me. What was I doing? It really hit me hard on that plane. And I was too far gone to turn around and come back. Everything was set up.

I flew back March the 9th, 1970, and we recorded it March the 10th. The luggage went back again. My clothes got lost, and I didn't have nothing but what I had on, and my shoes was killing me. But late that afternoon, before I went down to record, they found 'em, so I had a change of clothes before I went. The recording guys was real nice to work with. They liked the song real well and got to kind of giggling around about it. It was a lot of fun after I made up my mind that I really had to settle down to business, 'cause I was scared then and my mouth was dry as powder, and it was real nerve-wracking until it kinda got on its way. The sounds they was coming up with I really liked.

Then about the middle of April, somewhere about the twelfth, the record was released. We had only ordered a thousand copies of it. I didn't know what we'd do with a thousand records, 'cause I thought, you know, that they'd just be laying around. But that was the least that we could get made. Then my publisher called me one day, and he said, "Boy, your song's playing like crazy." It just started going real fast. The juke boxes started calling for them. So we ordered another thousand. My publisher had taken them around to radio stations, see, and they was playing it. My husband and I picked up some records. I don't know how many, but quite a number of them, and sent

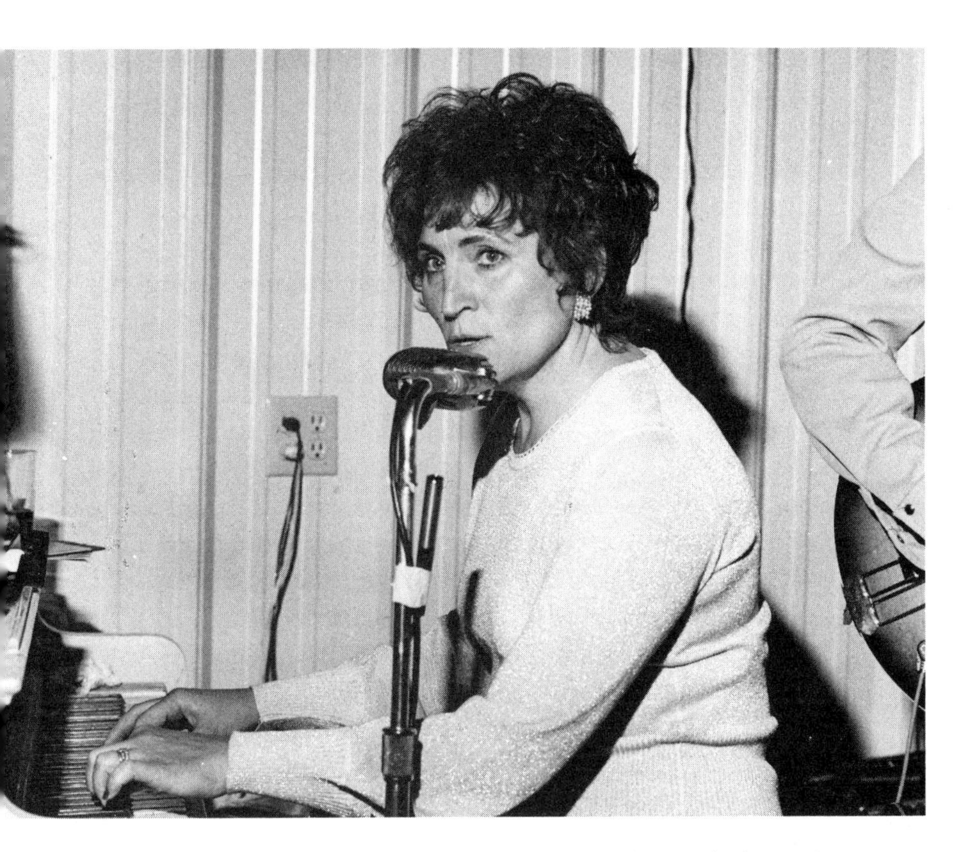

them to a lot of different places. I was real timid about it, 'cause I didn't know whether they wanted to put me on their juke boxes or not, and I give a lot of them away just to see if they even wanted 'em. Well, they started playing them. One lady, she laughed about it, but she said, "These kids would come in and get some money and play it time after time after time again." And she said, "I really like the song but I was really getting tired of it." I didn't blame her for that. (She laughs.) But it was kind of a thrill, too.

The newspapers started calling me wanting a story on it. And I was always scared about something like that, because I was always afraid I'd say the wrong thing. Disc jockeys would call and say, "Is your dad really a preacher?" They wanted me to comment on it. And I received letters back from quite a lot of places all over the United States.

Then in September, September 25, is when I found out that this other girl had a recording out of my song with her name on it as writer. That afternoon, there comes a phone call from a disc jockey and he says, "Turn the radio on." And they played several songs, and then the disc jockey announced, "Now this is the BIG ONE!" And it was my song, only she was singing it and her name was on the record as the writer, and there was another publishing company's name on it instead of my publishing company. Well, my publisher immediately contacted his attorneys, and they wanted me to come up with my copyright and things, which I did. Well, then the Nashville attorney called me, and we went back there. They seemed to think I had no problem and not to worry, 'cause I had the copyright, and I had even received royalty checks from the song. I paid them $1,250, and they said there would be no problems to it. They said it wasn't an infringement. It was a complete steal. That's how they described it. I wouldn't have minded her singing it . . . I liked her singing and the music. I was just trying to get established at writing.

Well, then things kept on happening. They told me there was a common law copyright, and that this girl had people that would go to court and swear that they knew she wrote the song before I did. And it really sort of scared me out. 'Course, everybody told me they're bluffing you, but you don't know what they'll drag in against you. And I couldn't figure out why my copyright wouldn't stand up over anything she had. It *is* my song. Definitely. But they advised me not to go to court, 'cause it would cost me so much and there'd be a lot of trouble getting all these people into court and everything. So, first thing I knew, I was out of it. They wanted me to forget it.

See, these are awful big companies, you know, for me to try to take care of my own song. I would have to have an exceptionally big strength, one who would stand behind me. I've contacted people all over, everywhere. And then my friends contacted people. Everybody says they can't do this to you. But they did.

I'll tell you. I was scared and worried. I couldn't eat and I couldn't sleep. I didn't know what they could do to me, being such big companies. And then my attorneys started telling me what might happen to me. I thought they was on my side. When we was back there, they was very nice to me. "No need to worry. You've got the first copyright. You've got everything." Then the last few times I tried to call them, I couldn't never get through to them. They sent me a contract to sign giving the other person and her husband one-third each and leaving me one-third of my own song, saying that I had agreed to this. I never signed the contract. I'll take all or nothing. 'Cause this song is just as much a part of me as my own flesh and blood.

I got to see her once. In the middle of all this, my doctor scheduled surgery for me. So I ended up in the hospital up in the city for ten days. And she happened to be there at a club just a few blocks away from the hospital. And my husband come in the morning I was coming out from under the anesthetic, and he said, "It's a rumor that this girl's in town. Would it make any difference to you if she was?" It just seemed like her name flashed across the wall. And I opened my eyes up, and I told him I wanted to know more. And he said, "It's a rumor that she's playing down here at the club." Well, he had found out about it the night before, but he didn't tell me before I went into surgery. After all that time I looked and looked and looked for her, and then we end up in the same city at the same time.

So I was settin' there real blue, and I wanted to see her so bad I didn't know what to do, and yet I was scared. I didn't know how I'd feel or how I was going to get down there. So I called my doctor, and I said, "I want to go down and hear her sing tonight." And he said, "You have my permission. I'll call the head nurse." So he called the head nurse and okayed it. So they got me ready, rebandaged me, fixed me, cleaned me up. And they took me down the emergency elevator, and my husband was waiting out in the car for me, and I went by the motel and I put on my wig and went into the club, sat down, and they was playing a real slow song. Then they came on with my song. Immediately. And that's one of the hardest things I ever did. Sit there and listen to 'em playing my song. Claiming they wrote it. I had called my attorneys from the hospital, and they told me not to talk with them or do anything. So I sat there, and my heart was just about to pound out.

I had to leave then. I had to be in the hospital by eleven o'clock. So I went back to the hospital, and I went in and took off my clothes, took off my wig and set it on top of this lamp I had at the corner of my bed. (She laughs.) And I got back in bed and I lay there and thought about that. From the hospital bed to the nightclub and back to the hospital. It seemed unreal. But I was fairly satisfied. I got to see her, and she came to my table, and they had some pictures of her, and they got her to autograph one. I felt in a way that they possibly knew me, 'cause they watched me all the time, but I don't know.

It's been a regular hassle. There's not a day that passes that I don't go over the whole thing in my mind. You see something that's out of your control that's yours. I've always been someone that's what is mine is mine, nobody else's. But this was mine, but it was also in the other girl's name. I'm scared of almost anything, in a way. And yet, I've got determination to go on because I like to write. This is a big world, and you never know what you can get into.

SUNDAY

Like the school, the Spa Hotel, the new community building, and some of its parishioners' houses, but unlike the other churches, the Methodist church is built of brick. The brick is fine old red brick, and atop the roof is a handsome white steeple with a belfry. Like all the other churches in town, the Methodist church conducts a Sunday school for adults and children, a regular Sunday morning and evening service, a summer Bible school for children, an annual fund drive, a teen program, a hospital visitation program, and a missions-abroad program. The interior of its sanctuary is a pleasant blend of light oak and red brick, white linen and shiny brass, stained glass and plush red carpeting. There are no flags or patriotic bunting, but there is a certain stuffy formality in the service: organ preludes, preselected hymns, responsive calls to worship, The Lord's Prayer, tithes and offerings, scripture lessons, sermons, responsive closing prayers, organ postludes. After Sunday morning service, everyone fellowships and munches cookies and sips coffee in the rear of the sanctuary. The coffee alone sets the Methodists apart from the Baptists and the others for whom hell is no mere metaphor.

Of course, some would say Methodists can afford to be liberal. Some would say they could care less about being born again; they just need a place to parade their finery and to look respectable on Sunday mornings. And there they are: the grain elevator manager, the air sprayer, the big irrigation farmer, the gravel-and-concrete man, the variety store owner. They have the brick. The biggest homes. The furs and dresses and the new Levi leisure suits and Tony Lama boots. The private airplanes. The bridge club ladies who play Wednesday afternoons in the winter and nibble nuts and mints. The sororities that raise money for Main Street's Christmas decorations. The new pickups, the land, the hired men, the kids who drag Main in the fanciest cars. In short, the Methodist church is the type of place where Al the Cowman, who wouldn't be caught dead inside any church any Sunday morning, feels quite comfortable watching his nephews and nieces getting married on Sunday afternoon. Al would be out picking shit with the chickens before he'd let his kin get hitched in a Baptist church.

Alva Dodd doesn't need the alarm clock to wake him up. He is up and dressed by six. The bedroom is at the back of the double-wide trailer home. Alva unconsciously checks the alarm setting for Millie, goes to the bathroom, urinates (doesn't shave), peeks back through the bedroom door (Millie rolls over in sleep, sighs contentedly; she will be up at six-thirty, have breakfast on the table an hour later), pads in stocking feet to the door, pulls on boots. The cooler was on all night and Alva leaves it on. His two black mutts dance excitedly about his feet as he walks past the weedy garden and the hen house up to the barn, gets in the pickup. The dogs jump up over the tailgate, stand with forepaws on the side panels between five-gallon diesel buckets, baling wire, empty oil cans, spare batteries, log chains, tool boxes, trash, shovels. Alva keeps the windows rolled down. The pickup's radio brings him static and undertones of gospel services from many miles away.

He drives slowly along bumpy field roads. His corn is well up. One of his better stands. The cattle peacefully graze last year's irrigated wheat stubble, fenced with hot wire.

In the next half hour, Alva checks the oil levels in his three irrigation pump engines (his father is going deaf; Alva now wears earplugs when tending the giant, raucous motors); closes sixteen gates and opens sixteen new ones on the gated irrigation pipe strung out at the high end of the furrowed corn fields, using a shovel blade to open and close gates, to dig starter trenches for water to flow into new furrows; sets a new drop dam to ditch-irrigate a patch of oats where the pipe won't reach, palming and setting tubes in the furrows; walks into corn rows to see how well the aerial sprayer dispatched the weeds; milks the cow; then turns the outside hose on his face and arms to cool (he is sweating heavily by seven, his faded pink seed cap darkened about the brim, shirt sticking to his chest, tan muscular arms glistening), removes his boots, pads through the house to bathroom, shaves, bathes, combs his hair back with water, and puts on a Sunday suit and city shoes.

Millie has started the living room cooler, over which hangs a crude commercial carving of the Last Supper. There is a jumbo blue-covered King James Bible with a white felt marker on the coffee table. Over the piano, Jesus in chiaroscuro, with long yellow hair and beard, white robes. On the card table by the door, an anti-obscenity petition and leaflets from the Billy Graham Evangelistic Association (Do You Know the Steps to Peace with God?). At the breakfast table, Alva says grace in a singsong cadence, hurried but gentle and soft: Father, we thank you for this food and this wonderful day we ask you Father to give us the strength to do your will and Father we thank you for the weather and the crops which have given us this food we eat in Jesus' name we pray amen. Millie serves out their own milk, butter from their milk, grape preserves from their arbor, bread from someone else's wheat (but from their oven), bacon cured from last year's hog, eggs from the hen house. The television brings blurry gospel to the table. At nine o'clock, Alva and Millie get in the car and head to Community Baptist, the smaller Baptist church in town, where they each teach Sunday school to pre-teens.

At 9:30 Sunday morning, twenty-seven pickups, including Al the Cowman's, are parked outside the Hitching Post; three pickups are parked outside Boston's Drugs (sundries and a few Denver newspapers on sale); fifteen wetbacks are drinking Pepsis and doing their laundry in the laundromat (there is no Catholic church in town); and Pastor Mackey of the big First Baptist Church is at the wheel of the baby-blue First Baptist Church school bus, heading back to town after having gathered children and old folks from the country. Everywhere, pursuant to the competitive codes of economic geography, Sunday school will begin at 9:45, just as Sunday morning service will begin everywhere at 10:45. It is about as hot as it ever gets this early on a Sunday morning in August, about eighty-five degrees. Almost everyone perspires, even young children. The wind blows steadily from the southwest. It brings dust, but no relief from the heat. The sun is so hot the earth, the streets, the buildings all look white. Bleached.

At 10:45, the pickups outside the Hitching Post have dwindled to a dozen, but there are seventy vehicles parked diagonally on both sides of Main Street in front of the First Baptist Church, fifty in front of Community Baptist, fifteen in front of the Wesleyan Church, and twenty-five in front of both the Church of Christ and the Methodist church. All the Sunday school classes have broken up. At Community Baptist, Alva Dodd posts attendance: 62. At the First Baptist Church, Brother Stinson, a local colporteur and church elder, posts 139.

Over the front door of the First Baptist Church there are a large picture of an opened Bible and big cursive letters of blue-tinted neon tubing spelling out JESUS SAVES. The exterior of the church is sparkling whitewashed stucco. The interior is a vast, make-do lecture hall with green indoor-outdoor carpeting in the aisles, linoleum floors, varnished blond-colored pews, big glitter letters in various places (over the altar, WE WOULD SEE JESUS), an upright piano, an organ, frosted multicolored glass in high side-wall windows, a state flag, an American flag, a raised pulpit with microphone, an open Bible and plastic floral arrangement in front of the pulpit, and hanging neon light tubes. There is no great formality for the 10:45 service at First Baptist. As the pews fill, female faces and white heads predominating, parishioners stand in casual groups and visit quietly. Although the program sets forth aphorisms, not an order of service, and although creased Levis and western shirts are as common as leisure suits, there is order.

Brother Stinson, colporteur and elder, takes the pulpit. Pastor Mackey (everyone calls him "Mack") seats himself, legs crossed, on the first choir bench behind the pulpit. The choir goes forward. Sister Marlene goes to the piano, Sister Donna to the organ. Brother Stinson calls out hymns and leads with flashing director's hands and a mike-amplified baritone vibrato. He Lifted Me. He Lives. When All God's Singers Come Home. All five verses are sung and, if necessary, all six. *Con brio.* Then there are birthdays. While Brother Stinson holds out a miniature steepled church piggy bank, those with birthdays come forward and drop in love offerings, in return receiving Scripture-engraved pencils. The congregation sings:

> Happy Birthday to you,
> Only one will not do,
> Born again means salvation,
> How many have you?

Reluctant to surrender the pulpit, Brother Stinson reads a brief poem. Or ad-libs a brief story. Or shares a brief passage he has read: something light and pithy, something to draw a few smiles, the warm-up before the big act ("Say, Dad, did you go to Sunday school and church when you were a boy?" "Yes, Son, regularly." "Well, then, I don't guess it will do me any good either!").

Pastor Mack rises, goes to the pulpit, adjusts the microphone. Pale complected now, he still has a farmer's open face, for his boyhood was spent on the farm south of town, and today his father is a church deacon. Mack wears the same western-cut suit every Sunday, along with cowboy boots, a necktie, and a bronze belt buckle with a horse's head engraved on it.

A month before my seventh birthday, at a revival meeting, the pastor in this same church was preaching the word of God. That men are sinners, and that the man who does not place his faith and trust in the Lord Jesus Christ is condemned eternally to separation from God in a place called Hell, which is a literal, real place. Well, my heart was tender and I didn't want to spend eternity away from God. So in a simple, childlike faith, I went forward and asked God for forgiveness of my sins and all that was displeasing to Him. And asked Christ to come in and be Savior and Lord of my life. And I know, personally, that I became a different person because of the attitude and the desire and the directions of my life.

Pastor Mack communicates (does not read, rattle off, or mumble) the week's announcements: Bud Arthright in hospital, pray for him; twelve-year-old Winnie Carson still in coma after horse kick to head, pray for her; remember teen pizza party next Saturday, Wednesday prayer service, family retreat in March, it will be a blessing to your heart. He then calls on Sister Marlene to play "Heavenly Sunshine" (Hallelujah, Jesus is mine!). Everyone stands and greets a neighbor or two. (Mornin', good to see you out! How ya doin'?) Then the offering. Checkbooks tear; coins jingle; some eyes are averted from the plate. It is 11:15, time for a special sing by someone from the congregation, usually the three Willberry sisters in silver-pure gospel harmony or Mrs. Yost in an erratic soprano that makes children fidget. This week, Will Schmidt hobbles forward, dragging his artificial leg. With his personal hymnal open to words he does not consult, with his mane of iron gray hair and his head thrown back, Brother Will belts out "The Old Rugged Cross," Sister Marlene speeding up and abating on the piano when Brother Will falters. Midway through, Will's voice cracks. He pushes his spectacles up his nose, gazes out at the congregation, shakes his head. "This old cold," he explains. Pastor Mack smiles. Will shakes his head again, nods at Marlene, and hurries through the rest of his number. It is 11:23. Pastor Mack is ready to preach.

Most people in my church have held me when I was in diapers. Now for me to be their superior, so to speak, in the matter of leadership, would be a traumatic thing for them. Unless it was something that God definitely established. And I think the scriptural principle is: when you humble yourself, God will exalt you. It's slower here. Preachers come in and want everything to change in six months or a year. You can't do that if you want a lasting ministry. If you're patient, and if you win their respect, it'll mushroom later. It'll be the difference between growing a corn stalk and an oak tree. You can grow a stalk of corn in four months, but the wind can knock it down in a day. If you want to grow an oak tree, you may take ten years, but the first wind that comes along is not going to blow it over. So that's the kind of leadership I strive for as a boy coming home to preach.

But this I say, he which soweth sparingly shall reap sparingly; and he which soweth bountifully shall reap also bountifully.

Pastor Mack begins: Imagine a farmer with a bin full of seed wheat. Excellent seed wheat. The best high-yield, semi-dwarf seed wheat. What if he didn't really plant it? What if he only pretended to? He worked on his machinery all winter. He got everything in tiptop shape. Come spring, he went to the fields with his plow, but he did not set the plow to the ground. Up and down the fields he drove. Then he hooked up his drill. He put the excellent seed wheat in the seed buckets. And he went to the fields again. But he did not set the drill to the ground. He made his sweeps, but nary a seed did he plant. At harvesttime, he has nothing to reap, nothing but weeds and volunteer wheat on his fence rows. But out he goes, up and down the fields with the combine, returning time after time with an empty bin. Crazy? What do you think? Think about yourself. Most of you are saved. You will sit at Christ's feet on Judgment Day. You will go to heaven no matter what you do. But only the wheat seed which dies produces more kernels of grain. You must truly die and be born again. And when you die and are born again, your work has just begun. You must plant yourself in the world. You must sow yourself. Then only shall you reap. Are you the farmer who only pretends to drill his excellent seed wheat?

The tempo increases. The voice level rises. As it is written. Verily, verily, I say unto thee. None righteous, no, not one. Except a man be born again, he cannot see the Kingdom of God. Faster and faster, louder and louder. *Except a man be born again.* They say: You've got a lot to live, and Pepsi has a lot to give. Well, you do have a lot to live; and Jesus has a lot to give. They say: The life expectancy of Americans is increasing every year. Is it? What do you expect? Do you expect to go to heaven? This may be your last opportunity. There may not be a tomorrow. For he that believeth not, the wrath of God. The lake of fire. What do you expect? (The question is left to hang.)

And now, as Marlene plays through the invitation theme, all heads bowed, all eyes closed, no one looking. Christians are praying.

(Marlene plays the invitation theme on the piano.)

Won't you come? Won't you come to Jesus today? Let him show you the way? There may not be a tomorrow. There may never be another opportunity. All heads are bowed, all eyes are closed. Christians are praying. If you have been moved this morning, if you are tired of the life you are living, if you desire to rededicate yourself to the Son who shed His blood so that you might have salvation—won't you come? Won't you come?

(Brother Will Schmidt and ten others go forward.)

There may not be a tomorrow.

(Marlene completes the invitation theme.)

Christians have been moved. The coaxing is done, and Pastor Mack shifts his voice tone. ("Brother William, will you dismiss us in prayer?") Brother William, feedlot cowboy, mumbles a prayer inaudible even to those in the pew in front of him. When the mumbling ceases, Christians stand, stretch, and blink their eyes. Smiling sleepily at friends and relations, they ooze out into the aisles, drift to the door. Pastor Mack's spell will last until they hit the sunlight outside. And the wind. The dust.

Will Schmidt: Can't Anybody Beat the Lord

The Schmidt residence is sixteen miles south of town, seven east. We drive down at dusk, and the farther south we go, the sandier the soil, the poorer the crops, the more fields blown out. The house is set back off a dirt county road in the middle of nowhere, a leaning two-story affair with no storm windows or weather-proofing. Behind it is a large metal round-top. Mrs. Schmidt, the second Mrs. Schmidt, lets us in. Will is lounging in a recliner in the living room, dressed in a farmer's coveralls and a blue work shirt.

He is sixty-two, and he talks readily about his childhood. "Them years, it was depression all the time. Never did know nothin' but. We was wheat farming with horses and mules. Farming was all we knowed. We just got by, that's all. Lived on bread and gravy. Had potatoes probably. For fuel, we picked up cow chips, cow manure." He usually wears his artificial leg, but this was a tiring day and Mrs. Schmidt told him not to bother. In the middle of the interview, when he decides we should all sing some gospel, he drops out of the recliner to the floor and crawls to the piano bench. He calls it "the pie-anna."

Growing up, we lived in a one-room dugout. Just a hole in the ground, the walls cemented up, built up about four feet on top of the ground with boards. Five boys and two girls was in the family for years.

I was married in '36. I had to borrow thirty-five dollars at the bank. It was my first note. (He chuckles and looses an impish grin.) We had a real celebration. We went over to Richfield, Kansas. My dad was on that WPA a little, and we farmed a little broomcorn together. We never did eat prairie chickens, but we'd eat old jackrabbits that didn't have no bumps on 'em. I started farmin' for the government payment. Plow up that land for probably a dollar an acre, just to keep it from blowin'. Then I started buyin' land. The land started about four dollars an acre. I bought quite a little bit. I could have bought three times as much as I did, if I'd just done it. Could have got it for ten cents, fifty cents an acre at one time. But then I didn't think I should. I've been up and down so many times, and I'm down right now. I started runnin' cattle probably about 1940, 1941. That's where I made quite a bit of money. Runnin' 'em on fields and farming and then the government payment. I was farming big.

Before I accepted the Lord as my Savior, I got pretty bad to shooting dice and gambling. A few times, I had loaded dice used on me. And one time, some of my good, crooked buddies kept giving me some bad liquor and beat me out about seven or eight thousand dollars one whack. Then I accepted the Lord, and I really quit it.

But this cattle feedin's a lot worse than gamblin' ever was. I bought cattle five months ago. I give thirty-four cents a pound for the cattle. Put 'em in the feedlot. Then I suppose fat heifers was abringin' about forty-three cents a pound. This evening I got a bid on them for thirty-three and a quarter. I told him I wouldn't sell 'em, but I got to sell 'em next week, 'cause they're getting over-fat. That's the kind of deal you've got, you see. And if that ain't worse than a dice game, I'll eat your hat.

I started drifting away from the Lord and got in the

wrong bunch. I never thought about the Lord for years. Finally, my first wife, she got saved and turned to the Lord, and then I turned back to the Lord and quit drinkin' and gamblin' and started back goin' to church. Like I tell people, well, they might not need the Lord too bad now, but if you have a death in your family you gonna need the Lord. You goin' t' need him bad. An' them loved ones goin' there, they need him real bad. An' you're goin' t' need the Lord t' getcha through it. But if you don't believe in the Lord, well, you ain't got nothin'. If you don't believe in the Lord and the hereafter, you ain't got nothin'.

When my wife died, I thought I's goin' to bring her home from the hospital, an' I walked her back from the hospital, 'cross the street. She fainted in my arms, an' me an' another guy put her back in bed, an' she's dead in four minutes. She had a blood clot. Then I thought the world was comin' to an end. First thing I done then was, I went in the bedroom there an' prayed. Then I got up an' I thought about how ol' Joe was there in the hospital. I'd been a-tryin' to get him t' accept the Lord. Old Joe was in there, an' he'd been burnt real bad. An' while I was in there prayin', the doctor came in an' kneeled down there with me an' told me how good of a patient she'd been. I got up from my prayer, an' I decided to go in there where Joe was. Joe asked me, "How's Maude today, Will?" I said, "Well, she just went t' be with her Lord a little bit ago." So old Joe, I guess, like to fell out of bed. Then I waited around there; the ambulance come and hauled her away. If I hadn't had the Lord then, I believe I probably would of went and got drunk.

We both want to ask him about his leg but don't know quite how. Jessica finally asks him bluntly what happened. He does not hesitate to tell the story, but first he gives a demonstration.

He rolls up the pant leg of his coveralls, leans back in the recliner, and sticks the stump up in the air. The skin is milky white and hairless. There is a large purple scar where the knee should be.

It was three years ago. I've got an elevator over here, east of town. We had a big auger running, running wheat out of this bin up in another one. I was with my youngest boy. It's running pretty good. I told him, I says, "Jimmy, you go ahead and eat dinner." He was in the office. "I'll go around there and check it." I had cowboy boots on, so I went there in my car and it wasn't running quite fast enough to suit me. I stuck my boot up there, my foot, I had a piece of tin up there over this auger, and when I did, well, it caught the toe of my boot in this auger. And it just started to draggin' me in there. Just drug me right in. I thought I's just going to be ground up alive. Well, there was a five-horse electric motor on the auger, and there were two belts on this thing, except one of them was broke. Well, I just thought, well, this is going to chew me up. Just draggin' like that. Don't think I wasn't calling on the Lord. And all at once, it quit, see? Broke the other belt. So I went to yellin'. Jimmy heard me. The office was sixty yards or so from where I was at. So he came out there, and the wheat was running down, just about to cover me up. Boy, I never was in such pain in anything. Between a-prayin' and callin' on the Lord and Jimmy and gettin' him to pray an'. . . . I told him, well, "Go call the gas station and have 'em to bring a welding torch out there." So he went back to the phone, and I laid there. The grain was a-coverin' me. Probably twenty minutes, they had the ambulance out there an' Doc Pete, an' they had the welding torch. The first thing I told the doc, I think I told him, "Doc, get to prayin'." He's a prayin' man. He turned his back and shoved somethin' in my neck. They got me out. I didn't know what's happenin'. Put me in the ambulance. I asked Doc Pete, "Are you still prayin'?" "Yes, I've been a-prayin' all the time." I asked ol' Bernie—he put me on the stretcher—I asked him, "Are you prayin', Bernie?" He says, "Yeah, I've been prayin' all the time."

So they got up there and put me in the emergency room. I knowed both of the nurses real good. I told them both, "Get to prayin'." They says, "Well, we already are." I guess I had to have more people prayin', I mean, than any other thing else. That's all I wanted 'em to do. They worked on me. Finally, I set up there on the bed, and Doc Pete, he says, "Well, Will," he says, "it ain't so bad nowadays. These artificial legs. They make some pretty good ones." I looked at old Pete. I says, "What do you mean? You done got my leg cut off?" (He laughs.) He says: "Yeah, we got to cut it off." I didn't know it, and I'd never been out. But I guess that's why I stood it so good. All them people prayin' on me.

Before that auger stopped, I knowed I's already meetin' my maker. After Jimmy got everything done, he laid up there with me. I says, "Jimmy, you prayin'?" "Yeah, I've been a-prayin' all the time, Daddy." I says, "Jimmy"—he's given me quite a little trouble in his life; he run off a time or two, wouldn't stay in school, and he give me lots of worry—I says, "I'll tell you what, Jimmy. I get out of this alive," I says, "I'm going to love the Lord better." He says, "I am too, Daddy."

I was in the hospital about a couple of weeks up there. I don't know. I had a spell in there. I got depressed. I couldn't hardly take it. My doctor thought I needed a psychiatrist, what do you call them? So they took this old psychiatrist in there. He talked with me a little. Got me in a wheelchair. Took me to a room. So he's talkin' to me, an'

I wouldn't talk with him. Finally, I got to talkin' to him about the Lord an' things. So anyway, he made a date for me to come down to his office. So I went in there, and we wasn't talking, so I just started talkin' to him 'bout the Lord. An' well, before I left I says, "Will it be all right to have a word of prayer with you?" He says, "Yes." (He chuckles.) He says, "You don't need me." He says, "I need you." I don't know about them psychiatrists. But I'll tell you what, I'd rather have the Lord any time than one of them guys.

Really can't anybody beat the Lord. When Jesus could die on the cross, someone die for us an' then he was raised from the dead, they can't beat that, can they? Knows the beginnings and the ends. A lot of times I haven't really trusted the Lord like I should. I'll admit that. I forget an' let the devil get hold of me an' forget the Lord.

I thought I was goin' t' meet the Lord when that ol' auger was a-grindin' on me. Boy, I never was in such a pain. And afterwards, it was just like the old foot and everything was on there. They'd give me a painkiller, but that'd keep a-going.

I like to sing gospel songs. I sing good enough for the Lord. The Bible tells you to sing praise to the Lord. That's what I do. Sunday morning we watch a lot on television. We watch that Larry Jones and then that other program from Cathedral of Tomorrow. It is really a good gospel program. Next one after that we watch "Old-Fashioned Bible."

Used to, I'd drive them old tractors, I'd be a-probably thinkin' about all the time what I was gonna do the next day. Plannin'. This year, I drove a pretty new tractor, and I took my tape player with some songs on it, and I'd praise the Lord. I'd sing with that tape player. Sometimes I'd hook it in and sing with that. Then I'd pray awhile. I'm thinkin' on them kinda things a lot more as I get older. A lot of times I get in pretty earnest prayer. Praying for my kids. They don't go to church very good, and I'm pretty concerned about that. Since I've been living for the Lord, when I run a tractor, I'll sing quite a bit. I'll get out there on that ol' tractor. If I can remember the words, I can keep in tune with it pretty good. The trouble is, I forget the words, you know. I get pretty high out there sometimes.

But as you get older, you know, your thoughts have begin to change, 'specially when you get a bunch of grandkids. We've got about fifteen grandkids, me and my new wife together. You get to thinking about them. Thoughts are runnin' a lot different than they used to be. I've had some pretty close calls with death, too. And we've had quite a few deaths in our family.

Six months after my wife's death I met my new wife. She wasn't goin' to church then. That's the way I met her. She lost her husband. She was workin' at a little ol' dry goods store in town. I went in there one day to get a cap. She was a-waitin' on me. Then I got interested in tryin' to get her t' go t' church. I guess the Lord makes me think people oughta get saved, turn to the Lord. I got t' takin' her to church. Then wanted to marry her.

My mother, she'd get us kids all washed to go to Sunday school. Papa was a good man an' all that, but he didn't take his place as the spiritual head like he should. He had his hired help and all, tryin' to make a livin'. Worryin' to death to keep us from starvin'. That's where I got my singin'. Mama used to go around, sing songs. She'd get on that ol' washboard an' sing. She didn't need no song book, an' she didn't need no pie-anna. She could just carry a tune an' really do 'em good. She was just thirty-nine years old when she died. Papa had seven kids. My wife was thirty-nine years old when she died, and I had five. I know the Lord carried me through them times. He's able. I'd a-hated to went through 'em without the help of the Lord an' the comfort of the Lord.

I was tellin' Jimmy yesterday. I says, "I didn't really think after Mama died, Son, I'd ever want t' marry again. But the Lord knows about what we, me and you, needed than I did. You never woulda had a mama." The Lord knowed more about what I needed than I knowed myself.

8 ❧ Best of Times, Worst of Times

Adapt or die.

EARL L. BUTZ *to the American farmer in 1955*

When the banker says he's broke
And the merchant's up in smoke,
They forget that it's the farmer who feeds them all.
It would put them to the test
If the farmer took a rest,
Then they'd know that it's the farmer feeds them all.

Populist song, 1896

BEFORE THE STRIKE

In 1929, the town is three years old. Council votes to impose a mill levy of five mills, issues six thousand dollars of water bonds, authorizes the purchase of three 150-watt lights for Main Street, and pays Virgil Olsen ten dollars for killing ten dogs, plus thirty cents an hour for his trouble.

Then forty-seven years pass.

In 1976, the town is fifty years old. Council votes to cut back the mill levy, and it is still the highest in the county.

The sewage pond is running over, the state doesn't like it, and the town faces a new sewage assessment of $3.50 per month per hookup. The kids dragging Main are getting so bad a rumor starts at the liars' table that council is going to buy a traffic light. The police chief, on the average, puts five dogs to sleep each month as part of his regular duties, all for $8,400 a year.

The town today is 385 water hookups, 900 residents, and 375 acres of platted ground. Council is six elected members serving two-year terms and one mayor. It takes council approximately three and a half hours a month to run the town. It also takes a part-time town clerk, a full-time street-and-alley man, a part-time maintenance man, a full-time water man, a part-time police judge, and a full-time police chief. At 7:30 P.M. on the first or second Monday of each month, council assembles at the firehouse. Or on the third Monday of each month. Or of every other month. Or at 8:30 or 9:00. It all depends on when Mayor Clem Harding can round up a quorum. Coffee is served, except when the pipes freeze and no amount of heat tape will thaw them out.

Them senior citizens meet at the hospital but don't think they should have to pay any part of the water bill for the damn meeting center. But the drunks meet there too, and by God the drunks got to pay. [The drunks are otherwise known as Alcoholics Anonymous. The Seniors make Christmas decorations for the town and want to use the community building at no charge.] Let the senior citizens off. All they get is that little bit of money from one of them damn government outfits. Hell, seems like they all want a free ride. Let 'em have it. It's decorations for the town.

Been gettin' a lotta kick 'bout this horn honking late at

night on Main Street. Damn kids. Get that new law off his butt. Been gettin' a lotta kick 'bout the water man drivin' 'round in the new town pickup with that big ole dog of his in the cab; they wanna know who's gonna pay to fix the seat. Water man: If that seat's hurt, by God, I'll pay it outta my own damn pocket. That's good enough for me. How much we gonna pay the street-and-alley man this year? I heard they're payin' nine thousand up to the elevator. Really? You bet. Better replace that transmission in the water truck. Them gears is finisht. Place over the state line, sell you one of them rebuilt ones for three-fifty. Gahrunteet. Ole Ogle down to the garage'll install it cheap.

Ed Williams and his mom have a kick about their water bill. Ed gets his back up and comes to council mean enough to run at a buzz saw. He and Councilman Daniels get into it. The other councilmen stare at their hands and sketch milo pastures on the margins of old newspapers. Ole Daniels gets madder than two tomcats with a knot in their tails and chews on Ed quite a bit. Mayor Harding says he'll work it out with Ed later. Ed says that ain't no better'n hot owl shit.

The kids come in. This new law, he's makin' us go home at ten week nights. What's that curfew deal s'posed to be, anyway? Where are the ordinances? Must be lost. Why don't you kids come back later? (After the kids leave, curfew is changed to eleven o'clock week nights. If their mommas and daddies don't care where they're at, ain't nothin' we kin do.)

This new police chief. Keeps makin' these long-distance calls on the town phone. Took some of them leftover Christmas decorations, too; put 'em up 'round his house. Mayor to chief: What do you think? Well, I use my house as an office. You could use the old jail. Sure, and you could put some heat in there. What about this back-up policeman deal? It'll be free. Free? Yeah, state law-enforcement training funds. Hell, he's already got his wife and kid helping him. His kid? Yep, damn kid's been givin' out tickets. Seen him myself. Chief claims he's done deputized him. By God, this little ole town don't need two laws runnin' 'round. Don't need that damn speed gun, neither. Well, we gonna buy it? How much? $949.28. Ain't gettin' my vote. Hey, how come you got so many hours this month, Chief? 341. Well, seven dogs put to sleep; two family fights; one burglary; five citations for horn honking after curfew; eleven dog bites; ten vehicle safety stops;

one accident, no injuries; and Fred Bertram's steer calf run over east of town.

Hear the sheriff's been usin' ole Pete Wilson as a special deputy for the county. Hell, we fired ole Pete last year. Maybe better get that damn sheriff over here next time and chew on him a bit. Born and raised here; moves over to the county seat and forgets his origins. Hell, thought we'd plumb defanged ole Pete.

Better get on that old well house down south. Gonna have a fire again. Call that carpenter down here and ask him how much he wants to do it.

Buck Jones comes in with a map. He wants his trailer court annexed to the town. How do them damn annexations work, anyhow?

Arla Benson won't pay for rodding out his sewer line. Cut off his water. Cut off ole Ed Williams, too.

That land we gotta buy for the new lagoon, the ole boy owns it says he'll work with us. How much he want? Dunno. Says he'll work with us.

That damn horn honking. Wife can't hardly sleep.

Gettin' a kick.

Take it up later.

In the county there is no such thing as an impersonal bureaucracy. There is no such thing as a political party. There is no such thing as an agricultural self-help organization. The intensity of people's aversion to organizations of all types is matched only by the depth of their ignorance about how to deal with organizations. If you have problems, someone in the family will help, or a friend will help, and the family member or friend who helps will probably be the assessor, the banker, the sheriff, the manager of the grain elevator, or the water commissioner.

In this self-determining, self-made society affiliations

with the institutions and government programs of the broader society are kept to a minimum. The county accepts federal disaster payments, price supports, and soil conservation allotments; it accepts the nominal designation of candidates for county commissioner as Democrat and Republican; and it accepts a state-supervised court system. But it deems state and federal political campaigns irrelevant, even at the peak of the campaign season in the rest of the nation. A political issue becomes a popular cause only when the churches decide to take an interest; the churches opposed the Equal Rights Amendment, and the county was one of the few in the state to vote overwhelmingly against it. Candidates for county office annually address three questions: whether the county dirt roads can or cannot be better graded; whether the assessor can or cannot be kept out of the coffee shop; and whether taxes can be reduced. Once elected, county commissioners, treasurers, sheriffs, assessors, and clerks stay in office as long as they choose, barring their infelicitous confusion of a basic ministerial obligation with the authority to meddle in the personalized system of community rights and duties.

Just over the state line, there are co-ops whose member-owned and member-operated enterprises pay big dividends and centralize marketing; they build local shopping facilities, gas stations, and garages, and promote limited block-marketing programs. The co-op in the county seat, however, is in the red, hasn't paid a dividend in recent memory. Just two hundred miles to the north, farmers since 1968 have been responding to the astute, dogmatically collectivist market-blocking campaign of the National Farmers Organization. Barely three hundred miles to the east is the small immigrant community of wheat farmers that inculcated idealism and ambition into the current president of the National Farmers Union, the agricultural flank of New Deal liberalism in America. Not too many hundreds of miles to the southwest, fruit and vegetable agribusinesses are uniting in conservatism and profit under the banner of the American Farm Bureau Federation. But people in the county will have none of it. Why would anybody want to organize to market his product? If prices are bad, you tough it out till next year. If you're a good farmer, Banker Johnson will work with you. If you're not, you ride it out on the coattails of your great uncle or your dad. Organizing just means some labor leader's going to cheat you in the end.

The county's judicial system, neither revered nor understood, is under-utilized. This is not so much because it is distrusted as because it fills no need. A state judge rides circuit into the county seat once or twice a month to sign orders or preside at preliminary hearings for hapless vagrants and roughscuff. His caseload of five hundred cases a year is half probate matters, handled by shuffling papers. Yet when cases do go to trial, the judge is well aware that once he crosses the county line at Big Horse Creek, county law prevails. Juries run wild; complaining witnesses refuse to testify; farmers ignore summons after summons for jury duty. The local-level county court, with jurisdiction over petty civil matters and criminal misdemeanors, is presided over by a practicing lawyer in the county seat; about four hundred of his five hundred cases per year are traffic offenses. Since the one other lawyer in the county is the part-time assistant district attorney who prosecutes traffic offenses, very few defendants obtain legal counsel. Plea bargaining is common, and plea-bargained sentences correlate reliably with the family name of the defendant.

In defiance of state regulations, the schools call on undegreed wives of coaches to substitute before they call on the college-educated wives of newcomer businessmen or outsider-farmers; but good coaches, properly treated, may stay a decade, while qualified teachers stay no more than a year or two. Al the Cowman drives with impunity up and down the county after his driver's license has been revoked by the state; but if officers of the sheriff's department or the state patrol stopped him, how could anyone legitimately expect to feed cattle locally? Farmers strip OSHA-mandated safety fenders from their combines before starting to the fields, even after paying a good bit extra because of them; but when you maybe haven't harvested for three straight years, missing fingers are of less concern than a missed crop. The sheriff and Immigration close their eyes when drunken wetbacks have to be locked up in the county jail overnight; if they went ahead and deported them, who would support the wetback's wife and six children left behind at Farmer Benson's place? Children of lifelong residents avoid prosecution for drug trafficking and vandalism; but in the perspective of the years prosecutions do nothing but drain an already shallow labor pool, while drug trafficking is cured naturally by supply shortages, and vandalism absolved pragmatically through restitution.

But organizational incursions into the county, if harsh and forceful enough, will be resisted. The people who resist are unschooled in meeting fire with fire—they cannot write intentionally ambiguous letters, jabber double-talk over the telephone, start countersuits, and hire lobbyists—but they can respond personally. Item: I am sitting in the law office drafting a will when the recently installed state electrical inspector walks in. He is furtive, his hands shake, he talks in scarcely coherent sentences. Although we have never met before, he takes me into his confidence. I'm not one of them; I can help. He tells how the state is having problems in the county and decides to appoint an outsider to be regional inspector. He is disposed to leave the city anyway, and he and his family begin to like the town. He enforces the state code rigorously but, he thinks, fairly. It isn't long before he discovers that two local electricians, who have wired every structure in the county for the last forty years, do not have valid licenses and pay minimal attention to code specifications. He is not long about his inspection duties, having disapproved a few new jobs, when the windshield of his parked car is blown out. He fixes it and continues to enforce the code. He is slugged on Main Street in midmorning by one of the electricians who's on a drunk. No witnesses can be found, and the police chief loses the investigation report. He continues to enforce the code. His car windows are shot out again, his rear tires slashed, and his children intimidated at school. He continues to enforce. His rear tire is shot out while he zips along a rural road, his wife has a nervous breakdown, and the state electrical board, after consulting the FBI and the governor, is about to transfer him to another jurisdiction. He wants to know what he can do. Legally. He tells me he was afraid to let his car be seen at the office, so he walked over. I tell him I'm writing a book. Legally, I refer him to a lawyer in the big city. In a few weeks, he and his family are gone for good.

Alexis de Tocqueville, who predicted that the richness of America's organizational life and the ubiquity of her opinionated newspapers would keep democracy from veering into tyranny, did not tour the new West. He did not tour the county, which wasn't even settled in his time. He never encountered these tough, unreflective people, who have guaranteed their freedom simply by banishing

Leviathan. He could not have imagined that flabby demagogues in the cities would one day identify these people as "rugged individualists" and plaster their faces all over billboards to sell cigarettes.

In the county, there is neither democracy nor tyranny, neither organizational life nor opinionated journalism. But there is still freedom. Months pass. Seasons merge. Years go by. There is no time, and because there is no time, there is no change. There is only place.

Representative Dawson: Big Duck in a Little Puddle

The first political meeting that I'd ever attended in my life was the night that I accepted the nomination to run for the House of Representatives. A few days before I was out in the field on a tractor, and my predecessor, a fella in the legislature, came out and said, "George, I'm not going to run anymore, and I want you to run." And I was elected. I won that one, and I've won every ten of 'em since that one.

His farm is in the county, but now it's rented out. Representative Dawson lives in the county seat of the next county north, in a large modern ranch house on a quiet drive off the main road, an appreciably shorter distance to the state capital. He takes us into a study whose walls are lined with twenty years of state political memorabilia: Dawson photographed with this and that governor, plaques from Kiwanis and various lodges, seating plans of past sessions of the House with miniatures of past members' visages blocked in. He talks freely and tends to ramble. We ask him why he ran in the first place.

I'll be honest with you in this. I got to thinkin' about it recently when I was asking some of these new freshmen why they ran. I think there's a number of things as to why people run. I think maybe an individual gets involved in something locally, or maybe on the state level, and they have an urge to get in there, and they really don't know what the process is till they get in there, but they're going to change this whole thing around. Then I think there are other people who have political ambitions, and they think this is maybe the rung up the ladder to higher offices in government. Then I think, and I think this is really why I ran for that office—and you won't believe what I'm going to tell you—but I think for me it was the mere fact that I wanted to be a big duck in a little puddle. I wanted to be a VIP. I think maybe I'd been in the state capital once before I was elected, and I was as far removed from that process as anybody could be at the time. But I categorize myself as the one who wanted to be a VIP. (He chuckles.) And I think you have to be a certain kind of a person. I think you've got to enjoy doing things for people. I get the biggest kick out of people coming to me and saying, "Can you help me?" And if I get it done, I get a great feeling out of it.

What was it like at first?

The first month I sat in that chair, I never felt so inadequate in all my life. Some of the old-timers came around and gave me advice; but back in that day, when you were a freshman, you sat in your chair and learned what the process was before you got up there and put your foot in your mouth on the microphone. And I did. I think maybe the first session or so I didn't even introduce a bill. Maybe I was only to the microphone two or three times.

My farmer-clients are feeling put out with the litigation process in their suit against the natural gas company, and they take a notion to come up to the capital and see if they can apply a little political pressure. Representative Dawson arranges a meeting with the conservative chairman of the House committee studying energy regulation. We all meet for lunch at a lounge near the capitol. The farmers drink iced tea, and Representative Dawson drinks what they usually serve in lounges near the capitol at lunchtime. He's had the farm rented out since 1970 and doesn't recall the last bill he got for irrigation gas. He and the conservative committee chairman talk to the farmers in generalities about the need to give the energy companies incentives to develop new fuel sources.

I used to be considered the most liberal rural legislator, and today I'm considered a very conservative Democrat. I've got Republicans on the other side of the aisle that makes me look like a John Bircher. I understand urban problems much better than I did fifteen, twenty years ago, but I don't think my philosophies have changed. And I look back, and I think it's probably that I've gone through knowing some of the real problems, people walking with pots and pans going to a soup line. I have a different interpretation of poverty than the general public of people today. I learned to sit up in the spring seat of a covered wagon, and I can remember when we got apples and oranges at Christmas and things like that. Got one or two new pairs of overalls a year. Walked or rode a horse to school. When my wife and I was first married, we had an outside toilet. We didn't have water in the house, and that was in the forties. When you wanted water, you went out to the well, and you took the lid off, and you got a bucket of water. During the Depression, I spent many nights out on that tractor that you didn't have a cab on it or hardly any fenders to keep the wheels from kicking dirt up in your face. No lights except for a homemade generator and battery. And the rollers. You'd have to hold a flashlight within about a foot of the ground to even see the ground. If anybody ever tells you a story about those kinds of storms, you believe it, because they can't exaggerate on it.

Most of the people down here went through what I went through. They're a different breed of cats, and I don't mean that in a derogatory way. They are self-styled. These are people who have climbed the ladder themselves with no help whatsoever. They're independent in nature; they don't want to be obligated to anybody. The old rancher-style people. When they told you something, that was exactly the way it was. My dad used to buy and sell cattle, and I saw him write a check on a piece of a brown paper bag one time for two hundred fifty head of cattle, and the bank paid it. Used to say: "If your damn word isn't any good, your signature ain't either." (He laughs.) But people grew up modestly, and that hangs with a person over the years. I don't think the average person here has changed his philosophy as other rural areas have.

How would you describe yourself?

That's a tough question. (He pauses.) I've been judged by so many other people. (He laughs.) Well, I'll tell you. There's one thing that I have tried to be all my life, and that's to be honest and straightforward with the people you're dealing with. A lot of times it hurts, and you have to bite the bullet. But I think . . . well, what do you want out of life? What do you want to get out of your life? Do you want to be of service to people or to your country? How hard do you want to work to make money? I've never had an ambition to be a millionaire. I've always wanted the better things in life, but I was taught that I had to work for it if I wanted it, that nobody was going to give it to me.

I guess I have worked hard in my lifetime, even at the job I'm in now.

I argue with my older brother. My parents had told me that it wasn't so, but my brother always told me, he said, "No, you wasn't born in the house. You was born in the barn." It was a half-dugout we had then, dug back into the bank down in this creek, and later on the folks built a house back up on the hill, and then they converted that dugout into a horse barn. So I said, "Well, our creator, Jesus, was born in a manger." (He laughs, then pauses.) When you just stop and think, I've served twenty years, 20 percent of this whole state's life, one-fifth of it. It doesn't hardly seem possible, but I have no regrets.

The American Agriculture Movement has taken hold. Several hundred farmers come to the state capital and blockade supermarket warehouses with tractors. Someone decides they should invade the legislature. They surround it, leaving their vehicles double-parked in the streets. They swarm into the chambers of the House and demand legislative endorsement of their goal of 100 percent of parity. The chambers have never been packed so full, and legislators are ashen-faced, nonplused. Representative Dawson watches and wonders.

REVOLT

The following article appeared in the county paper one day in April 1977.

A vast, multi-tentacled, economical conspiracy has so grasped the market control of our agriculture endeavors, that we will soon be left but two choices: To forsake our small fields and pastures, and with it our life's vocation, or submit to servitude as impotent tenant farmers.

We have witnessed for fifty years the struggles of the two great political parties for power and plunder, while grievous wrongs have been inflicted upon our agrarian society. We charge that the CONTROLLING influences dominating both parties have permitted the existing dreadful conditions to develop without serious effort to prevent or restrain them. Neither do they now promise us any substantial reform. They have agreed together to ignore every issue but one. They propose to drown the outcries of a plundered people with the uproar of a sham battle over government price supports, so that conglomerates, multi-national corporations, banks, trusts and the oppressions of the usurers may all be lost sight of. They have exploited the mass media to bring the wrath of consumers upon our doorsteps. They have secreted dissenters among our organization to keep us estranged, and preventing a united effort to secure an equitable profit for our labors. They propose to sacrifice our individual farms, lives, children on the altar of Mammon; to destroy the last vestige of agrarian free enterprise in order to secure corruption funds from the millionaires.

Wealth belongs to him who creates it, and every dollar taken from the farmer and rancher without an equivalent is robbery. "If any will not work, neither shall he eat." The interest of rural and civic labor are the same; their economic enemies are identical. We do not say one word against those who labor in the cities, but we who have made this the most food-abundant nation in the world—the farmers, ranchers and dairymen who followed the paths of our pioneering forebearers and reared our children next to Nature's heart, erected schoolhouses for the education of our young, churches where we worship our Creator, and cemeteries where we rest our dead—we are as deserving of the consideration of our nation as any people in this country.

The avarice conclave of market manipulators have manned the misfeasance battlements against us, and we are faced with an uncompromising war of survival. Our war is not a war of conquest; we are fighting an economic war in the defense of our farms, our families, our posterity and the natural right of men to receive equal value for the fruits of their industry. Individually, we have petitioned, and our petitions have been scorned; we have appeased, and our appeasements have been disregarded; we have even begged, and they have mocked when our calamity came. United, we will beg no longer; we will appease no more; we will petition no more. *We will defy them.*

For several successive weeks the articles continue to appear under the black, quarter-inch-tall heading REVOLT. The articles exhort county farmers to stand together "shoulder to shoulder to meet the dispossessors at the gate." The articles assert that normal political avenues of redress no longer work; that "international thieves" control monetary policy, and corporate giants have infiltrated the food industry; that the "Dollar Diplomats of Capitol Hill" have formed a "power structure presently controlling every fiber of America's economic life."

The articles are unsigned except for a mysterious reference to a "Name on File." We wonder who the author is. No name comes to mind.

One week an article poses the spectre of burning wheat fields and range-slaughtered cattle. It pictures empty granaries and "money changers . . . milling flour from the ashes of . . . smoldering fields." This is too vivid. A few restive but moderate farmers dispatch the county's intellectual, Mike Klimm, to track down "Name on File." Klimm visits the mystery agitator and tells him his calls to action are irresponsible. They detract, he argues, from the peaceful efforts of moderates in agriculture to help shape farm policy by working in the system. They undermine the county's image. Mike suggests that the prairie radical pack up his typewriter and leave.

The articles do not stop. We too seek out "Name on File."

Karl Billings: Make Them So Mad They'll Stand Up

Basically, what I'm trying to do in my articles is to educate the people in this county in the process of economics. To understand the international marketing system, the banking system, by some method to reach that inner spark in them, to stimulate them with fire and venom, to make them so mad they'll stand up. I guess I'm disillusioned. Up until a couple of months ago, I firmly believed if I was going to start a movement, I thought my own hometown has got to be the place. I thought, man, those rednecks out there'll fight. (He laughs.) Well, they're rednecks all right, but they're not fighting.

He was raised in the county, lived through foreclosures, including his father's. It soured and hurt him. "Every day, you sit on that tractor, and you see the cars and the buses go by, and you say, 'Some day, some day, it's gonna be me.'" He joined the Navy, kicked around in engineering for six or seven years, went back to school, got a degree in journalism. Just as we are preparing to leave the county, he returns, having lost a newspaper job on the West Coast after a fight with the editor about a "backgrounder" he'd written on agriculture. "I was frustrated. I started doing an awful lot of writing, and about two months ago, I came back to this county. I thought I'd come back home and stoke the coals." The tape recorder does not faze him. In fact, there is immediate rapport. We have one thing in common: the experience of life in the county and life on the outside. Is our conversation something like that of parents discussing a much loved but, alas, eternally immature child? Later, though, Karl confesses he had reservations about the city-bred lawyer and the Ivy League sociologist. Preparing some damn government report, maybe. He drinks coffee and smokes mild, filtered cigarettes. He is fortyish, balding, dressed in urban casuals. Outside, gusts of dry, swirling dust smudge the blueness of the June sky.

The small independent farmer is not very long for this world. He's a vanishing breed. In as short a time as ten years, five years if we have two more years like this, he'll be gone. There won't be any individual farms. It's going to be run by conglomerates. There'll be individual farmers, but they won't be any more than just tenant farmers. It's just pure economics. Farmers are getting less for a bushel of wheat today than they did in 1919. That's unimaginable. There's no inflation in commodities. The law of economics says that when you have inflation, it hits everything. But how in the hell can it hit something when it's twenty cents less in Federal Reserve notes than it was in real gold and silver in the twenties?

Today's farmer's days are really numbered now. Corporations are moving in like crazy. Farmers cannot compete with those people. You cannot sustain losses for fifteen or twenty years. When you're looking at land payments, cattle payments, equipment payments, it only takes about two years. You miss two years, and you're through. The bad farmers have already been eliminated. Now it's the good farmers that are losing.

The American farmer is gone, and there isn't anything that people like me can do except be prophets of doom. They might be able to change it, but they aren't going to do it. They hide under a bushel basket all the time. They see it happening all around them, and I guess they have to believe it's not going to happen to them. And by the time they're ready to fight, they've already lost everything. Why don't they do something? I can't answer that question.

I've been told by a number of people that they can't think of a radical movement that ever succeeded where it condoned a measure of violence. But, it seems to me, back around 1776 there was a radical group that raised a little hell, and they succeeded. When they tell me that student protests and the hell-raising of the sixties didn't change things, they're wrong. One of the strongest groups in agriculture is the Independent Milk Producers. And, by God, they were a little violent when they were turning over trucks and dumping milk.

It sounds pretty militant and radical, and I'm not an advocate of violence by any means, but there comes a period of time when you have to do something radical. I don't foresee anything happening unless they literally do something extremely radical. They can't even get the attention of the consumer right now, but if half of this county's wheat fields would go up in flames and smoke, they'd damn sure get their attention. I'd take half a dozen semis of wheat and drive down Pennsylvania Avenue and dump them. I'd have wheat on the capitol steps of every wheat-producing state in the country, plus Washington, D.C. And by the time a few senators and representatives walked through half a million bushels of wheat to get to Capitol Hill, maybe they would finally understand a little bit. The ghetto riots made people understand the frustrations of the inner city blacks. Maybe those people would begin to understand the problems of the farmers.

I'm told that if something like that started happening,

the whole damn country would go up in flames. Anarchy would reign supreme. (He sighs.) I'm not sure that that might not be better. I'm not so sure that there's a lot of our system worth saving. It's the oldest story in the world what a politician says and what he does. President Carter promised the American farmer that he would insure that they got the cost of production plus a reasonable profit. By the Department of Agriculture's own figures, $3.25 is the cost of production for a bushel of wheat. And he set the price for $2.37 or something like that. Lies. Rhetoric. Garbage. How many years can American society live being disillusioned every four years?

Not that I want government price supports or any of that damn garbage. Government should get the hell out of it and let supply and demand rule. I certainly wouldn't want more price supports. God, that's what's causing the problems that we're having right now. Farmers think that without price supports and things they're lost. But it's because of the damn price supports that they're in the mess that they're in right now. If agriculture had been totally government free, the price of wheat right now would probably be seven or eight dollars a bushel. Simply because the farmers aren't going to raise something that they can't sell. But with government price supports and subsidies, they'll plant every last acre that they got 'cause the government is standing there handing them the money. It's just a pure greed motive that makes them go out and plant ten times what they need to.

The agricultural community has never really developed a great articulate spokesman for their industry. There is no George Meany, John L. Lewis, Martin Luther King, or Cesar Chavez in agriculture. I can't imagine a segment of our society that is as large as the agricultural community without any leadership. You just think that sooner or later out of the backwoods, some great person is going to arise. (He laughs.) But I can't find anywhere in history where that's happened. There's potential leadership, but it's never developed. Had someone with strength appeared on the scene a few years ago, my God, what a political clout that would have been. But it just never happened, and now it's too late.

I guess if ignorance is bliss, they got to be the happiest people in the world. There's so much inner strength and fortitude in the average American farmer. They have more resilience than any other group of people I've met in my life, but there's so much ignorance, pure, unadulterated ignorance. There's a prevailing thread that winds through all of them that rejects education. There's so many things that are alien to them. You would think that when people make a living they would be so thoroughly informed in the methods of their area. But they have no idea of the factors that create the markets for their commodities. Or of our exports. Who controls their lives. They can see from that field to that grain elevator and that's the end of it. The farmer is trapped in a world that he can't control. He's the least independent person in the world.

Their organizational efforts have become a total waste of time. The ones that are large enough to be an effective political force are oriented toward things like insurance and showing dollars and nickels and pennies. They have an inner independence that won't allow them to reach the point where they'll do something for themselves. I don't know whether they can't face it or don't want to face it. And I don't care what they want to call it, but it's stupidity.

I don't say the things that I'm saying out of any disrespect for them or anything else. For God's sake, I come from a family where I had first-hand knowledge of going through three generations of heartbreak and frustration on the farm. My grandfather first came out here in 1912 and homesteaded, and they were able to survive for about two years and finally they were blown completely out, and they went back to Missouri. Then about 1926 or 1927, my mother and father returned and prospered until 1933. And they went three years without being able to raise a crop, and then the bank came out and foreclosed on them. So they struggled again, and in 1946 they were able to get back on the farm. Did all right the first year, and then they had a tremendous crop, and grasshoppers wiped them out. For the next two years, grasshoppers wiped them out. And since they just got back in farming, they had no assets to maintain themselves, and they lost out again.

When my father lost his farm, he lost everything. He was never the same man again. He had no more will. I've talked to people that were neighbors of my mother and father; and for that particular area and that particular time, he was considered a fairly prosperous farmer. And when the bank came out and foreclosed, they literally left them completely destitute. There were four kids, and they literally put them out on the street, and they literally walked from the farm to the town. I was nine years old. You see the things that were a part of your life up on the auction block. You see a man that you have all the love and respect for sit there and break down and cry. Turn his back and walk away. And even at nine years old, I knew that was the end of his life. Even though he lived for another twenty years, *that* was the end of the man's life. And that's hard. You never live that down, you know. But who do you strike back at? The bankers that foreclosed on him? Or the whole system which allowed it to happen?

I'm sure that a psychiatrist would go back and want to associate all my inner frustrations with that time period on. But it was destructive in more ways than just one. It destroyed our whole family. The whole family unit was dissolved. From that time on I grew up away from home with a sister and brother-in-law. It was after that that my father turned alcoholic, and he and my mother separated. It was just . . . it all went to hell.

People should go back and read John Steinbeck's *The Grapes of Wrath*. Lord, how many people have I known that were basically kicked right the hell off their land. And it's happening right now. It's not even the thirties, and they're foreclosing like mad.

Do you think people read your column, understand it?

(He gives a snort of a laugh.) Hell no, it's just an outlet for my own frustrations. I could never hope to achieve what I want to. Do you realize what it's like trying to write for this type of audience? When you really write what you want to write, in the way you want to write, forget it, because they cannot only not read it, but they cannot comprehend what you're trying to say. And when you write where they can understand, it loses its whole point. I use my thesaurus in just the opposite way. I go to the thesaurus to find a word that's simpler that means the same thing.

But you think the family farm is worth saving?

I don't know. Maybe it has no business in the twentieth century or the twenty-first century. You remember the things you want to remember. I still think in terms of twenty-five years ago. When I lived on the farm, we were self-sufficient. We butchered all our own meat, we always had turkeys and chickens and ducks and eggs and gardens. My mother canned everything, baked our bread. Our family had three meals a day, and everyone sat at the table and ate. Today, they just have their evening meal together, and they eat on TV trays and watch TV. Most of them, they're farming in terms of what material things they can acquire with it rather than out of any real love. I don't see that labor of love that I used to. It's missing. It's gone. I'm trying to recapture it, but it's an illusion I'm chasing. You can't save something that doesn't exist.

But if I didn't love these people, I wouldn't do it. It's surprising, the magnetism of this country. I'm not going to give up this effort till it reaches the point where I can no longer sustain myself. But maybe I'm thinking about saving something that doesn't exist anymore. There still is a rural family unit, but that thing is missing that it used to have. Rural people are becoming urban, not in terms of sophistication, but in terms of material things. Guys in town have fifty, sixty, maybe a hundred head of cattle, and where do they go to buy their meat? They don't butcher their own cows, they go to the supermarket. (He laughs.) Today the whole world comes apart when the television goes off. Right now, I've got two years where I can really give 'em hell. It's gonna be all over for the family farmer soon, but when the ship goes down, I'd sure like to see them have all their flags waving.

Epilogue: On Strike

Karl Billings misjudged his audience: they *were* listening.

For many American farmers, fall harvest in 1977 capped the third successive year of an economic bust. The three-year bust followed upon the 1973–1974 boom under Nixon and Butz, when record government subsidies and Russian wheat deals pushed consumer food prices to their highest levels in memory. Just how bad the bust had become in 1977 was revealed in a statistical report the Department of Agriculture released in September. Measured by the parity index, a ratio of prices received by farmers to prices paid by farmers related to a base period, August grain and cattle prices were at their lowest levels since the Depression. Wheat was down to 40 percent of parity; corn and milo to 48 percent of parity; cattle to 60 percent of parity. In its new farm bill, meanwhile, the Carter Administration was proposing a schedule of farm commodity subsidies geared more to pleasing the budget balancers than to taking up the slack in the depressed market.

Independently of each other, farmers around the United States in August and September of 1977 staged wildcat protest demonstrations against the perceived unfairness of the market and the indifference of the Washington bureaucrats. In drought-stricken Georgia and in the Red River Valley and in south Texas, they rolled out their tractors and paraded down the streets of nearby cities to show their dissatisfaction. In the county, too, there were stirrings. Several hundred angry farmers held a stormy meeting in early September, and there was talk of radical notions like going on strike for 100 percent of parity. The surprising thing was that the stirrings did not subside the way they always had in the past.

Something had changed. Characters as disparate as intellectual Mike Klimm and gruff Al the Cowman sat down together and cooked up handbills containing declarations of war on Washington. They took the handbills in their pickups to communities hundreds of miles away and gave them to over-the-road independent truckers to transport even farther. They lined up their tractors and combines and flatbeds along fence lines on the state highway and bedecked them with handpainted signs. THIS FARM ON STRIKE FOR 100% OF PARITY, the signs said. They said they wouldn't plant and they wouldn't market until they got better prices. When the national networks put them on the evening news, calls started coming into the county from as far away as Delaware, Minnesota, and California. Suddenly the county's protest acquired a national flavor. Somebody said they oughta go to Washington and demonstrate, and sure enough on December 10, 1977, thousands of farmers in big four-wheel-drive tractors rumbled through the streets of the nation's capital for 100 percent of parity. It was a miracle. But, by God, it was real.

If Karl Billings deserved the real credit, the county farmers never gave it to him. After they had christened themselves the American Agriculture Movement and taken over the little aerial sprayer's building on Main Street in the county seat for AAM's national headquarters, they gave Karl a job as press secretary. But nobody was too surprised when Karl eventually went on a drunk, hung some paper around town, and ran off with the wife of one of the protesting farmers. No, the rednecks were taking credit for this one themselves. It had taken them a long time to resolve to act, but when they did it was their show. They were as righteous and blind to their faults as the heroic inventions of a tragedian.

Since 1977, the American Agriculture Movement has become much bigger than the county. Half a dozen or so county farmers have survived the trials of television cameras, congressional committees, and Washington suitcase living to retain places in the organization's leadership. They are changed people, wiser and more disillusioned. So far Congress has beaten back their efforts to gain legislative endorsement of the concept of 100 percent of parity. On the other hand, they and their tractors have wintered on the Potomac twice, and they say they will return again unless they get what they want.

In the county, where out of respect to its origins the American Agriculture Movement keeps its national headquarters, a more familiar battle rages. Since 1977, the county has been visited by more devastating droughts and by a plague of grasshoppers. A cyclical upswing in the cattle market has boosted the fortunes of some, but the cost of natural gas has risen so high it has almost killed irrigation farming as the county has known it for the last twenty years. Grain farmers are dirt farmers now, but they are still a long way from meeting their costs of production.

There is some talk of building a gasohol plant in the county. A number of farmers have started participating in an AAM-inspired program to market grain directly to foreign nations. The Democrats swept the last county elections, but if anything the washboards on the county dirt roads are worse than ever. Boys' basketball didn't make it to State last year. It's a fair bunch, though, and this year they may. At the liars' table, everybody is saying how strong the wheat looks. *House Calls* recently played to an almost empty house at Abe Berkowitz's Ace Theater. The churches are having great success with their revivals, and every month or so a kid kills himself in a speeding pickup on the state highway. People marry and die and go insane. Hello, time. Good-bye, place.